Jonathan

The Letter to the Ephesians

ADRIENNE VON SPEYR

The Letter to the Ephesians

Translated by
Adrian Walker

IGNATIUS PRESS   SAN FRANCISCO

Title of the German original:
Der Epheserbrief
Second revised edition
© 1983 Johannes-Verlag, Einsiedeln

Cover by Roxanne Mei Lum

© 1996 Ignatius Press, San Francisco
All rights reserved
ISBN 0-89870-570-3
Library of Congress catalogue number 95-79947
Printed in the United States of America ∞

Dedicated in friendship to
Mother Dominique-François
and
Mother Marie-Dominique
Sisters of Bethany

CONTENTS

PREFACE

The present meditations on the Letter to the Ephesians belong with the author's other volumes of New Testament meditations by reason of their distinctive features. In the first place, her method of expressing the theological meaning of an enunciation is not merely to state the universal Christian truth but also to characterize the particular angle of vision from which the sacred writer sees it. The Johannine writings, upon which Adrienne von Speyr commented in their entirety, reflect quite consciously this disciple's mode of seeing; the same is true of the expositions of Peter and James—whomever we have to thank for the redaction of these writings attributed to the two apostles. Correspondingly, her commentaries on a few Pauline epistles—the First Letter to the Corinthians and the three prison letters—bear the imprint of Paul's way of conceiving the content and life of faith, and the self-conscious role of the apostle in the economy of salvation accordingly stands out in bold relief. These differences, which the attentive reader cannot fail to notice, stem, not from any psychological interest, but from a purely theological, more precisely, a "missional" concern: the "charisms" of the first great heralds of the New Testament message were diverse, in order that the contents of this message might be illustrated from various perspectives and thus be perceived in their inner fullness, indeed, inexhaustibility.

The second distinctive trait of the author's scriptural commentaries complements the first yet is somehow perpendicular to it: it is a distinguishing mark of all her writings that brings into prominence her own personal style of theological thinking. In the strictest objectivity, which concentrates exclusively on the word immediately under consideration and meditates on it without glancing either to the right or to the left, she aims to retrace the way through the content of this word back to the sources of revelation. Everything relating to anthropology points to some aspect of Christology, and everything touching Christology refers back to the Trinity as to its ultimate presupposition and explanation. The originality of Adrienne von Speyr is this unremitting, absolutely unswerving regress to the triune God, who not only occupies the central position in the whole of scriptural revelation but is its one and only viewpoint (*objectum formale*) and, at bottom, its all-commanding content (*objectum materiale*), the theme that must be heard for its own sake and that must echo through every other motif as through so many variations. And the authenticity not only of theological understanding but also of Christian life, of God-centered ethics, requires this reduction.

The insights that the author, by profession a physician without specialized training in theology, dictated to the undersigned are drawn solely from her contemplative meditation on the scriptural texts, and it is impossible to distinguish here how much her expressions owe to inspiration from above and how much they depend on her own prayerful reflection. The editor has altered nothing of what she herself said; he is responsible for the arrangement of the biblical text, for titles and headings, and for small grammatical corrections that were necessary on account of hasty dictation. For the second edition, a few minor stylistic improvements have been made and the title of the volume has been brought into conformity with the author's other commentaries.

Hans Urs von Balthasar

PRELUDE

1:1. Paul, an apostle of Jesus Christ by the will of God, to the saints who are such and to the faithful in Christ Jesus.

The Apostle begins with the address. And the first name to be mentioned is his own, because in everything he has to say he pursues from the very outset a definite course: his own. He will not cease saying in his own name everything he is about to say. Whatever he is going to announce in the name of the Lord, in the name of the Father, in the name of the Church, in the name of believers, will be marked by his personality. He is perfectly conscious of this; even the truth that is communicated in an unbroken way, as it were, from the triune God to man will unmistakably have his personal stamp when he explains it and in so doing makes use of himself in order to produce some effect in men. This will have a twofold quality: first, insofar as he is this unique *Paul*, next, insofar as he is *an apostle by the will of God.* He is never going to forget two things: that he is called and that he was called while still the sort of person he formerly was, that his vocation was equivalent to a conversion, to a complete change in the direction of his life. Consequently, he considers himself entitled, in fact, obliged, to pass on his own conception of Christian matters. He is the first among the apostles of Jesus Christ who speaks as a personality. Not only as inspired by God and endowed with authority like Peter, or in an almost superpersonal mission of love without fixed lines of demarcation like John, but in the full force and awareness of his uniqueness. The work he performs always remains his own work, within the commission God has conferred upon him. And after having said that he is Paul, he immediately says that he is an *apostle*. But his being an apostle is like a function of his being Paul. He is Paul, the convert, who day by day receives the gift of conversion afresh in his apostolate. Everything he does is always at the same time an act of keeping his conversion alive. He never distances himself from the moment when God turned him around. He grows, of course, and his insight and experience grow as well, but he remains in a freshness of faith that preserves the freshness and fragrance of new conversion. He lives in a sort of perennial conversion, as one who is always just now becoming an apostle.

He is an apostle of *Jesus Christ* and remains one. He will never be the apostle of some particular school, of a branch, but always of the whole unity of the incarnate God. His apostolate is one with his total bond to the Lord. During the entire course of his apostolate, he is never going to put any distance between himself and the Lord or estrange himself from him. He is never going to slacken, never grow cold. He will never do anything that would not find its explanation in the most direct connection with the Lord. For he became an apostle of Jesus Christ, not by his own will, which could make his apostleship depend at some point or other on his good will and his own judgment, but by the will of God, the triune God, who converted him while his own will was contrary. He has been chosen. God has fulfilled his will in him. And Paul always sees in this will the unity of two facts: the fact that he is Paul and the fact that he is an apostle. The manner in which he sees in himself the unity of the personal and the official is in some respect comparable to the way in which he sees how in God the Persons can be distinguished within the unity of the essence. Thérèse of Lisieux no longer sees herself as anything but a Carmelite as soon as she is in the cloister; she can often quite forget that she is Thérèse. Paul never forgets that he is Paul; the conjunction of the two elements is guaranteed him in the will of God. The accent with which Paul places his name at the head is entirely different from the accent of Peter when he does the same thing. Peter speaks in the character of the Church, within an almost impersonal mission that he had to assume as if by accident. Paul speaks with a much stronger accent out of a mission bound to his person, a mission that will have to be good for others because it is good for him. In everything he does and says, he must never be forgotten. It is as if in all his deeds and words he were demonstrating his own anatomy: this and this only is the way I am put together.

He became an apostle, not on his own initiative, but *by the will of God.* God's will intervened in his life and made him what he is. He knows, of course, that he was also Paul by God's will; but he knows even more that he became an apostle by it. He recognizes in it the same will that caused the Son to become man and thereby made him the master and leader of the apostles. In the one will of God are situated both the Incarnation and his own vocation. He, Paul, stands at the point where God the Father gave the Son the gift of the Incarnation and the winning of the apostles to his service. It is here that he knows with just as much conviction that he is Paul by the will of God as he knows that he is an apostle by it. His own becoming man (*Menschwerdung*, "incarnation") and his becoming an apostle lie hidden safely in the unity of the one will of God. From this point of view, one can say that he could no more not be an apostle than he could not be Paul. Just as in God's saving will the Son cannot be anything other than what he is: the man who at the same time is the Son. Paul sees in God's will the power that unifies everything and fits everything together, that permits nothing random or inconsistent to exist. This is so in his own case: through his being Paul we know that he is an apostle and vice versa. In the same way that with the Lord we can conclude from his being man to his being the Son and, conversely, can conclude from the genuineness of his sonship to the genuineness of his Incarnation. The one will of God is Paul's surety that he can be both things in one: Paul and an apostle. It is like the instrument by which Paul measures himself. For Paul is indeed a self-measurer, within his mission. He knows himself, he knows precisely where he stands, much more precisely, for example, than one of the evangelists. He does not merely have knowledge; it is also the task laid upon him to need to know, always to verify anew his station and its unchanging certainty within God's will. Other saints distinguish with easy readiness between their person and their mission, even between decisions they can make as private persons and those their mission requires of them. Paul cannot make any distinction here, just as there are often priests who can separate the personal from the ministerial only with difficulty or not at all. He thus becomes the paradigm of the perfect identity of being a man and being the bearer of a mission, which at all events is a specifically masculine possibility. The woman will always still know at some level how she is operating as a person; the male can let himself be entirely absorbed in actively working out his mission.

To the saints. Saints are those who believe. What Paul has to say in his letter can be addressed only to those who believe. Unbelievers would not understand it. In order to understand it, one has to have risked the leap into holiness, at whatever point it may be. Paul does not expect his letter to effect conversions from unbelief to belief but only conversions in the sense of a dilatation of believers' knowledge of the faith, of a will to greater surrender, to attempt a more perfect life in the Lord. Faith is the prerequisite; but faith understood as an exigency, not as purely theoretical cognition. Faith as an operative power that realizes an ever stronger unity between the content of faith and the believer. A faith, in other words, that has an entirely Pauline form, insofar as it is also always striving toward an already given unity, in the same way that Paul moves toward the unity of being a man and being an apostle, a unity that at the same time was always already his point of origin.

Who are such. A beginning, a spark of holiness must already be present in order for the conversion that Paul has in mind to work. Here it is not a question of the conversion from nonbeing to being. It is a question of men who already carry within them the ferment of faith that is destined to be developed to fuller life. The letter is certainly directed to a definite community, perhaps to the Ephesians.[1] If one were to add "in Ephesus" here, this would not be false from the point of view of the content; but in this context Paul means something else: he is relating being to being holy.

Many things in Paul seem abrupt. He has presented himself with great precision; one might have expected him to add a few words of explanation about holiness here. He does not do so. Whereas a John, proceeding from love, always gives the rudiments, which he then lets unfold down to their innermost core, Paul consciously begins at a higher level. He does not feel called to give elementary lessons in his letters. But neither can he refrain from noting it whenever he observes an offense against the rudiments in his communities.

And to the faithful in Christ Jesus. They are acquainted with a fidelity that they live by, and it is fidelity in the Lord. To be faithful in the Lord means to live in a sort of permanent state in which the image of the Lord remains steadily before one's eyes and determines everything. In this "fidelity in the Lord", it is the Lord who is the faithful one, and those who believe attempt to adapt themselves to this faithfulness and out of his fidelity to do what is asked of them. The fidelity of the Lord, which in man becomes fidelity in the Lord, is something given, just like

---

[1] Adrienne's text of the Bible reads "to the saints who are such". Some Greek manuscripts, however, may be read as follows: "to the saints who are in Ephesus".

grace. This fidelity does not yet say anything in and of itself about man's perfection, about the intensity of his faith, his will to surrender. It is like a point of departure, like the unity of the origin, which can both lead to perfection and degenerate into a state of lukewarmness. It is a living point, an initial capital, as is very clearly the case in a conversion. From that point on, one can continue to live in such a way that he merely allows the Lord to be faithful in him, leaving fidelity to the Lord alone, without summoning the courage to put it into practice himself. But one can also let himself be roused by the faithfulness of the Lord to fidelity in the Lord.

1:2. *Grace to you and peace from God our Father and from the Lord Jesus Christ.*

Paul draws a distinction between grace and peace. *Grace* is everything that comes from God and is intended for man, and in the eternal God this grace is undivided and perfect. It is the share that God the Father and God the Son and God the Holy Spirit keep ready for man in a never-failing attitude of readiness. Only by man's receiving it does it take on particular colorations. In God it is one and indivisible. If we perceive separated modes of manifestation in it, if the Church, following the Lord's instructions, classifies it in different species and distributes it into diverse receptacles, this happens because, as a result of sin, men are no longer capable of understanding grace in its totality, because, though not totally blind, they also no longer truly see. The grace of the particular sacraments now has diverse effects, and these are in turn different from the effect of those graces that God communicates directly, from the effect of a conversion, for example, or of a miracle or of thoroughly everyday graces. Had Adam not sinned, his whole existence, action and thought and experience would have been a single great grace, and he would have responded to this one grace of God in a single, undivided surrender. Today grace, insofar as it comes from God, is still whole, but with respect to its reception by the sinful world it must, as it were, split itself into facets; it has to strike us again and again in the particular, inasmuch as we have lost the eye for the whole and the readiness to receive it.

Peace is the working of grace in one who has received grace. It is just as necessary to the believer as grace. Grace springs from a divine "necessity": God wishes, according to his design, to give man enduringly what belongs to God himself. Man responds to this gift by receiving peace. Here peace means: enduring readiness in receiving, continuity.

The two terms have a much more official sense than in John. There they are like the pure expression of love, the pure flowing from God to man and from man back to God. In Paul everything shifts much more into the objective, from the human point of view at least—for the divine objectivity is love itself, and it is this that John speaks of. Both are objective, but in different degrees; they speak on different planes. John simply sets forth the highest norm; he leaves to others every accommodation of the divine to the dimensions of man, the Church, and the organizers. He is little suited to order and oversee human relations. Paul has this task assigned him. John may be compared to a man who has discovered a gold mine and announces the discovery; he is totally overwhelmed by the joy of the great event. Paul begins to turn the treasure to account in a rational manner, to calculate what can be done with it, to found, to cast, to mint coins.

From God our Father. Paul says this united with the Lord. God is the Father both of the Lord and of every single believer. There is a point where the distinction ceases to count (because the Lord no longer wants to make it), where the Father generates the Son in a perennial act but also graciously gives created man a share in this eternal, uninterrupted generation. But because the Son is God, the perennial generation of the Son is at the same time the Son's always being in existence already, whereas man truly does get to participate in this being generated but must do his own part to help the grace of generation toward full realization in him through the operation of the Lord, who is the Word. A child does not cooperate in his own generation. In the generation of a Christian by God, however, the Christian must have a part in the act of generation (by his own agency or, as a child at baptism, through that of the sponsor). The eternal Son lets himself be generated passively by the Father without actively contributing to it. Here he embodies perfect obedience, just as the child generated in the mother's womb is pure letting-be, pure obedience. But then he takes part in the generative activity of the Father in the generation of Christians. For in the world the Divine Persons work in common. The Christian who has attained the use of reason must himself—precisely because the Lord now takes part in the generation—make his contribution, expend every effort to open himself to grace, take pains to understand it, to allow grace to do its work in him. This collaborative doing is quite central in Paul. If he speaks little of merit, it is because he speaks that much more of effective performance, of work, of the active side in man, which meets the activity of God halfway. In the generation of the eternal Son this sort of activity is not required, because he is eternally one with the Father and is perfectly ready to obey the Father. We, on the other hand, are not at one with God and have to learn, as children of God, to become more and more one with him. If the Son is not an active participant in his own generation, however, then he is all the more so in ours: he takes over the most important part of our activity; he is already present in us in order to meet the Father halfway in us.

And from the Lord Jesus Christ. The Father no longer bestows any grace and peace now except together with the incarnate Son. If we receive a sort of insight into the grace of God, if we come to know something about its distribution, if we learn particulars that lead back into God's totality, it is because the Son takes part in this, because even as the Incarnate One he is not at a remove from any grace of the triune God. Before the Incarnation, God's Trinity was still undisclosed; only voices, visions, and missions revealed something of God, but these did not permit any insight into his inner essence and therefore did not definitively put man in communication with him. Thanks to the Incarnation of the Son and the saving work he instituted—the visible Church, the sacraments —the connection is established; first, the translation of trinitarian reality into terms we can understand; second, that active presence of the Son in us that enables us to comprehend God's grace and give it an answer. Even after his return to the Father, this extroversion of the Trinity is never suspended: heaven remains open from now on. Thanks to the Son, who is man, we are set on the right path toward God, even though the leap into God still seems like a leap into the unknown. If a distinction is drawn now between our Father and the Lord Jesus Christ, this is a sort of reassurance: we shall be able somehow to apprehend and understand this grace and this peace because the Lord has a share in dispensing it. It is he who knows, it is he who leads, and so for us he is the *Lord*. Lord just as much in our relationship to ourselves as to God. His being Lord is the expression of his obedience to the Father; as far as he is concerned, the Son would consider himself more as the slave and servant of God and men, but it is the Father's wish that the Son exercise lordship, and so he is Lord out of obedience to the Father.

THE PLAN OF SALVATION IN GOD

1:3. *Blessed be God, the Father of our Lord Jesus Christ, who has blessed us with every spiritual blessing in the heavens in Christ.*

We are able to bless God because we have been blessed, because by his grace we may give grace. God the Father has made this reciprocity a reality in his Son.

If Paul extols, praises, and blesses God right at the beginning of his letter, it is because this is one of the first things given to man so that he can draw near to God. He cannot do it simply by waiting; he must give. Give what has been received, which, as it passes through man, certainly no longer returns so radiant as when it set out. And yet it becomes radiant once again because its destination is God, because in this situation the recipient, God, confers upon this imperfect human blessing his own perfection, so that man need not be afraid to bless God but, in doing so, even performs something necessary, complies with a request on the part of God. Paul explains this blessing in greater detail when he adds:

God, the Father of our Lord Jesus Christ. He refers immediately to the relationship between the Father and the Son, because thanks to the Son we are in a position to bless the Father and to know him as the Father of the perfect Son. Our whole view of God is now determined by his property of being the Father of our Lord, and we bless him above all because he is this Father, because he has given himself up to us in his Son. Because he has made out of our life a sign of his life and through the Son has communicated to us the grace of being our Father in a new way. From all eternity he was our Father in that he created the world and us, but now through the Son he has become the Father of our new life, in which it is no longer we who live, but the Son in us.

Who has blessed us with every spiritual blessing. Everything in our life that merits the name blessing stems from him: both those blessings we recognize as such and the much more numerous ones we do not grasp as blessing. These blessings are *spiritual*, that is, blessings that the triune God, Father, Son, and Holy Spirit, bestows upon us, blessings that possess the perfect character of the triune God, of the invisible Father and of the Son who has become visible and of the Spirit of Pentecost. If we earthbound and sinful men can really represent to ourselves only as much of the essence of this dispenser of grace as the Son has shown us in earthly form, his intentions remain hidden to an even greater extent, as do the number of the blessings and their essence and the mode in which they operate. We know only that all these blessings are of a spiritual nature. But our spirit, though it does indeed receive a share in eternal life, is still so bound by our earthly body and its senses that it hardly reaches beyond what it can experience with them. The incarnate Son leads us again and again to a point where we can still just guess something of the supersensible and spiritual: through the miracles they see and hear, the disciples come to believe; through contact with the wounds, Thomas sees into the divinity of the Lord. Thus, the senses help the spirit to grasp the eternal, but the spirit cannot yet free itself from the senses in order to be totally in eternal life. As long as we are on earth, we will never lay hold of the fullness of the spiritual blessings that God pours out upon us.

In the heavens in Christ. The fact that God blesses us in the heavens is a consolation. For on earth we do not have the capacity to see the fullness of the blessing—any more than we can the whole of grace. But if God has blessed us in the heavens, we know that this blessing is adequate to the heavenly reality and to its dimensions, that it is an eternal blessing. And again: in order that we not be lost in the eternity and infinity of this blessing, he has blessed us *in Christ,* which means that he has concretized his blessing in his incarnate Son, so that we might thus become capable of comprehending something of him. In heaven, everything would be incommensurable for us, both the blessing itself as well as the exigency it includes. In the Son everything becomes in some sense commensurable. The Son is, of course, God and fulfills his mission in a divine and infinite way. Yet there are concrete, comprehensible things and aspects in this mission: one sees how he does and accomplishes divine things as man and how he can be imitated. This also consoles us in the face of the heavenly incommensurability of our mission.

1:4a. *As he chose us in him before the foundation of the world, that we might be holy and blameless before him.*

God has chosen us, and has done so in his Son, as if in this act of election he had placed his Son between himself and us. And this is before the foundation of the world. Even then the Son was the way without which no one comes to the Father. This is not a truth that became true only with the temporal Incarnation; it already counted as a truth before the world was created. God chooses us in his Son so that he can see us in his Son and through him. It was never intended that the eternal triune God would stand on one side and that we, creatures and sinners, would stand alone and unprotected on the other. Rather, from the very outset the Son was slipped in between as the one in whom we were to be chosen, destined as the one in whom we were to be created and redeemed. If God had chosen us, as individuals or even all together, without sliding the Son in between, we would now be nothing before his face except what we are, sinners. But God intended to see something else before him, namely, the *holy and blameless.* But he can see us as such only if we become such. However, we cannot become such by ourselves but only through him who is such: the Son. The holiness and blamelessness of the Son is so great that it is sufficient to make us, too, appear holy and blameless before God. And, vice versa, the greatness of God's grace can be estimated by the fact that the unique holiness and blamelessness of his Son are enough to make the enormous mass of sinners appear holy and blameless in his presence. And this was so even *before the foundation of the world*, as a sign that God the Father was all-knowing and all-provident. Hence, in the creation of the world, he did not leave us exposed but had already chosen the one who was to save us. This choice in which the Father chose us in Christ is irrevocable; it precedes everything else, even the question of whether man will fall or not. Had Adam not fallen, then he would have been holy and blameless before God, and we cannot say that the Son would then have had to become man in order to guarantee by this expedient the holiness and blamelessness of Adam before God. Perhaps he would have become man only to recapitulate the whole creation in himself, to raze completely the boundaries between heaven and earth, to establish full unification between God and man, to introduce us into the vision of the Father through himself, not as redeemer, but as consummator, by placing us at the point where the vision from the world to the Father and from the Father to the world is one in himself. This, however, is not what is in question here, but rather the fact that God's immutable will, providing for the eventuality that we would fall into sin, holds his Son in reserve from the very outset, so that, should the need arise, even sinners might appear before him as holy and blameless in the Son.

Holy means: living by his life. *Blameless* means: not living by our sin and our possibilities to sin. Living exactly like the newly created Adam, who knows only what God gives him to know and who does not know anything that does not come from God. The holy and blameless Adam knows that the serpent does not come from God; but the sin begins where, in spite of that, he yields to the serpent. Holiness and blamelessness do not exclude knowledge about what is not of God. It rules out only experiencing it, receiving it, obeying it. Holiness is participation in God's life; the contrary would be incipient participation in that which is of the serpent. One may indeed know about the serpent, but at the point where it does what is opposed to God one must not join in and must hinder what it is doing. Herein lies once again the anti-Quietistic dimension, the active aspect of Christian life in the Pauline spirit.

1:4b–5. He predestined us in love through Jesus Christ to be adopted children for him, according to the good pleasure of his will.

The word love is now mentioned for the first time. In everything that concerns us, the eternal will of God was love. Love that derives from God's love for his Son and, moreover, can never be separated or differentiated from this love. And so that God would have no need to separate and distinguish here, he gave us to his Son from the very beginning, so that we might be holy and blameless in him. If he had not always taken this precautionary measure from the very first, we would have made a joke out of his love by our sin. His love would have appeared changeable to us. Because this love shares in the immutability and eternity of all that he is, however, and in order to preserve love's divine quality for all eternity, God had to secure it through his Son against all the attacks of our sin.

And he *predestined us to be adopted children.* Just as he saw in the eternal Son his child, his idea was to see also

in us, his creatures, his children. We are destined to become his children through the eternal Son, because we
were unable to remain in that condition by ourselves.
God made Adam his child, just as he wished to make
all Adam's posterity his children. But because Adam fell
and dragged his posterity into sin with him, adoption was
no longer possible except *through Jesus Christ*, who never
sinned or distanced himself from God. Thus, through
Jesus Christ we now become children *for him*, that is, because the Son fetches us back in such a way that for us
being continually fetched back like this becomes a permanent quality, in that we abide in the return movement
without being able to transform it into a definitive state
of having arrived. As Christians, we must know that until
the end of the world the Son will be continually in the
act of fetching us back, that he ceaselessly carries it out
for the Father.

   According to the good pleasure of his will. The Father's will
is presented at this moment as if it belonged to him alone,
distinct from a possible will of the Son or of men; and
this aspect is necessary so that the Son, and we together
with him, can submit ourselves to this will. We must be
obedient in order to be brought to the Father by the Son;
and so that this obedience might become comprehensible
to us, so that we might understand it and at the same time
understand its opposite, disobedience, the Father gives us
the prototype of the perfect obedience of the Son, who
knows no other will than to do the will of the Father and
who thereby traces the path for our own will and in a
certain sense fetches us back into the Father's will, which
is his own will as well. On the other hand, the Father

is perceived only through the Son, and he has the Son proceed from himself in order to reveal his fatherly will in the Son. This will is at the same time *good pleasure*. Its sole content is what is intended for his own joy, but this is a joy that includes the joy of the Son and our joy at the same time. Which means that from all eternity the creation of the world, the Incarnation of the Son, and our sanctification in him were designed to serve the purpose of giving pleasure to the triune God. But also that from all eternity this pleasure was not a joy God wanted to experience and enjoy for himself alone, but rather an open, communicated joy.

1:6. *To the praise of the glory of his grace, which he has graciously bestowed upon us in the beloved.*

We cannot be children of God in the Lord without simultaneously being assigned a task and a corresponding empowerment. Otherwise our status as children would not be active, it would not really belong to us; it would be a mere title, not a truth. Implicit in our state of grace is a mission. But as the former has its place in the Son, so too our mission as children of God cannot be situated anywhere else but in the mission of the Son, in participation in it. The mission of the Son does not stop with him; it passes into the Father. For this reason the final goal of our life of adoption is also the Father. And, according to God's eternal designs, our purpose and our mission are to be his children to the praise of the glory of his grace. We can do nothing better than to fulfill the intentions

God has for us: we thereby fulfill our purpose, our *raison d'être*, and, accordingly, our being.

The Son came in order to glorify the Father. We have come in order to praise the glory of his grace. That marks the distinction between the mission of God the Son and our mission as believers. The Son glorifies the Father directly by means of his entire life; we glorify the Father by praising the glorification of his grace. The Son, who even as man always remains God, sees and comprehends the Father while he glorifies him on earth. We sinners, in contrast, can neither see nor comprehend the Father, and our service can only consist in the praise of that glory and glorification that has become visible in the Son. The Son realizes the whole mission entrusted to him by the Father; as God-man, he is one with this mission. We men, however, while striving toward the Father in the Son, attempt to glorify him by our praise. And that which we are able to glorify of God is above all what we have received and can perceive, that is, what is accessible to us of him: his grace. We could say that the Son glorifies the whole Father and that we glorify the grace of the Father, the Person of the Father who has turned his face toward us in the Son, the Father whose turning to us we grasp only in his grace. The Son alone has the comprehensive view of the whole Father; we must give the Son credit in order to glorify the Father. He assures us that the Father as a whole is as glorious as we possess and sense him to be in the grace that has been bestowed upon us through the Son. Here the Son assumes in toto that position of which a share will later be entrusted, in the Church, to individual saints: to impart a comprehensive view.

The Father has given us grace in his Son chiefly because he has gathered all the grace that is due to humanity—is due to it according to the good pleasure of his grace—into him. Not as into a closed vessel, but into a center of focus from which all the rays proceed. The Son perennially dispenses the grace that the Father keeps in readiness for men—nothing less than the whole plenitude of fatherly grace—to such an extent that there is no distinction between the grace of the Father and that of the Son. It is only through the Incarnation that the vessel of divine grace has become accessible and visible to us. God took this route via the Incarnation to found the very possibility of our seeing a way to him at all.

In the beloved. From all eternity the Son is the beloved of the Father. But he is the beloved inasmuch as he fully reciprocates the love of the Father. Between the initial bestowal of the Father's love and the answering love of the Son, there are no gradations, there is no diminution. They love one another with the same love; the particular fatherly quality and the particular filial quality of the divine love in no respect alter the fact that the love of the Persons in God is consubstantial. It is this love that the Father reveals in his incarnate Son and in this revelation also communicates and gives. Now, however, the incarnate Son will respond to the paternal love with divine and human love at the same time; and his human love will be so drawn into his divine love that it cannot be considered a diminution, an eclipse of the divine love. In Christian love, whose archetype is the Son, the entire energy of human love derives from the divine love. The work of the Father's grace consists precisely in giving man the gift of being able to respond to him with the whole radiant purity of supernatural, divine love. Wherever original sin and man's actual sin do not cloud the relationship, man need not feel distant from God on account of his creatureliness. God is not like a sun that is capable of emitting only weakened rays into its world. He bestows in grace an unbroken participation in his goods. The love of neighbor brought to us by the Son is, when it draws its strength and substance from the triune love of God, no different, newfound love, but the love the Father shows the Son and which is now streaming out into the universe.

Through the Son's grace it is possible for even us fallen men to become partakers of perfect love. At the instant the Son accepts our fallen human nature and raises up our groping, feeble love to the perfection of his own: at this very moment one may speak also of our perfect love. For the rounding out of our love by his gracious love gives it the quality of the divine love, and on the strength of this quality our love can and must be termed perfect. Christian love cannot be just an objective state of grace in the soul, for love is always something subjective as well; and the subjective element that corresponds to the objective perfection of sanctifying grace in us is nothing other than perfect love for God and neighbor, which, however, can live only by the Son's grace-filled love for us. In this Christian love there comes a moment when we are no longer outside but inside the divine love, when our living and loving are flooded through and through by the divine love, when what is ours no longer lives except from what is God's. From that point on there is no longer anything human that might stand independently over against God, for everything human has been assumed by the Son and, in order to be understood, has to be explained by the center—the Son, who is equally God and man and, in both, *the* beloved par excellence.

1:7. *In him we have redemption by his blood, the remission of sins, according to the riches of his grace.*

Paul now explains why we have become holy and blameless through the Son. We are so because the Son has redeemed us by his blood. By the whole of his blood. The redemption was already established when he became man, that is, flesh and blood. Already at that moment his blood was the blood of redemption. Through the shedding of it on the Cross, it was shown that all the Lord's blood was reserved for our redemption. He assumed it solely in order to be able to shed it, in order to give it to us as a gift. The redemption did not consist merely in the fact that he paid off out of his own capital a debt charged to our account. This was not the principal meaning of the shedding of his blood, but, far beyond that, this act embodies everything the Father in his grace had intended for us in the way of participation in heaven. The Son does not merely perform the work of redemption. He is, as the beloved of the Father, the redemption in person; he contains it as he contains his blood, in order to communicate it to the world by shedding it and, by this shedding of himself, to give the world the holiness that is the holiness of God himself. The one who wanted it so is the Father; he places his holy Son before us, so that we might become holy through him. In the Son he has summed up everything he desired to give to the world: holiness, grace, eternal life.

In the abstract, God could, after all, have created a second Adam, could have, so to speak, started his creation once more from scratch. But the Son placed himself at his disposition, in order to be this second Adam. From all eternity, in fact, he possesses the same will as the Father, and when he becomes man, he will be able to set forth and realize on earth that being which the Father had in mind at the creation. The blood of the first Adam was indifferent; it could flow in the direction of good or of evil and be used for either. The blood assumed by the Son of God, on the contrary, is not indifferent; it is from the very outset the blood of a redeemer, blood that is to be shed in love, which therefore contains the fullness of holiness, just as the entire flesh, the entire human nature of the Son is also earmarked for the redemption. It is no indifferent flesh and blood that is subsequently sanctified by means of right use or of some blessing. It is holy flesh and blood essentially and from eternity. The holiness of every human body is measured by whether it is assigned a space within the Lord's mission of love, even if it is a mission of suffering, sickness, and death.

Whatever the Lord did on earth, whether he was a child or fasted, prayed, was tired out from preaching, relaxed with friends, conversed familiarly with John, sweat blood or hung, on the Cross, he did everything while continuing to carry the blood of the redeemer. He was aware of this continuity and of the redemptive meaning of his life down to the smallest actions. He regarded his body and blood solely as a tool that the Father had given him for the redemption of the world. Mary knew only from the moment of the Son's conception on that her body was in such a continuity of service. She bore the blood of the redemption in herself, and while doing so she came to understand that her own body was holy; that her entire service in the body—during her pregnancy or in the household or in the service of the Cross, in every service that was asked of her—was always service of God. She understood that there was nothing in her body, whether hand or face or any other member, that belonged to herself, because everything was harnessed into an uninterrupted service of the Father, of the Son, and of the Holy Spirit. For the sake of this service, she kept her body holy, she dealt with it as befits an instrument one does not use for one's own ends but in order to serve someone else's wishes. The Christian will order his relationship to the body taking his lead from the experience that the Lord and his Mother had of the body. What the Lord knew in the eternal divine decree of the Incarnation, what Mary learned through her motherhood, he has to learn through Christian stewardship of the body, perhaps best of all by practicing bodily penance: that the body, whatever use it is put to, will always have to be an instrument of the Christian's mission. Ultimately, all Christian missions in the body—whether joyful or painful—are included in the blood of the Lord, which has been given us by the Father. This thought should educate Christians to great simplicity and naturalness in everything having to do with the body.

This redemption through his blood is something *we*

have. It is something we possess. We are chosen by God in order to receive it, but we also actually possess it. It is true that we receive it continually as something new, that we do not possess it outside the act of receiving. But the act of receiving ends in every case with a genuine possession: by permitting us to live in the Son, God gives us a title to partake in what is the Son's. What we receive is not perpetually withdrawn again. God does not give his gifts while constantly threatening to take them back again. What he gives as a gift, he gives wholly and definitively, asking only that in order to keep the gift we remain where the gift is: in the Son.

But in him we have not only redemption but also *the remission of sins*. If we remain in him, if we remain where he redeems us by his blood, we are released from our sins. They are not only forgotten or not imputed to us, but —what is far more—they are remitted, separated from us, taken away from us. They are banished to the place where everything God does not want and condemns is: hell. That is their place. In the history of the fall and redemption, it is much more necessary that such a place exist than that it not exist, for it is the enduring witness to the remission of sins. In this sense hell is even a gift of divine grace. If the remission of sins were their mere annihilation, any continuity in man's life would be finished; the sinner of before and the justified man of now could not be called the same man at all; more than anything, however, the gift of grace could not become operative in him, for there would no longer be any starting point for understanding what it means to receive grace.

Redemption by blood and the remission of sins both

have the property of being permanent: they are a step, a movement, a process, and their certainty and irrevocability are not incompatible with the fact that we never leave them behind. In Paul this process is influenced by the negative point of departure to a greater degree than, say, in John. In John, the redeemed man is simply drawn into the light of God's love. And the remitted sin lies at his back. In Paul, remission is an objective step whose measure is always codetermined by that from which one has turned away. Because remitted sin has its place, there can exist this kind of relation to it, and, thanks to this relationship, remission perpetually remains an ever-present happening. Paul can as little get over this wonderful fact as he can ever get over his conversion. With some saints holiness always springs anew as a reception of grace from the lived experience of conversion, of the remission of sins; not as if sin could become a cause or an occasion of holiness; but the degree of sin reached can serve in grace to make the love of the convert well up with perpetual freshness out of his contrition and out of the remission of sins. No one may sin in order to have a deeper conversion; if, however, he has in fact sinned, grace is so great that the gravity of his sins is, as it were, added as a factor in the weight of redemption. And because sin has a place, the one redeemed who remembers it knows that it has a part in all sins but also that the Lord's remission is equal to all sins; he, the redeemed, thus receives a share of heaven through the redemption, just as he once had a share in hell on account of his sin.

According to the riches of his grace. We cannot guess the measure of these riches, because they are entirely in God, that is, equally in the God of the eternal life we do not see as in the God of the fleshly and temporal life that, having appeared visibly, we have seen. If we attempt to get an idea of redemption by his blood and of the remission of sins, we are again and again forced to refer back to the criteria of our humanity, in order thereby to learn what it means to be exceeded by grace. But we know that we cannot in this way grasp or even have any sense of the largest portion of grace, because the greatest grace will be the vision of God in eternity. As long as we do not possess this vision, we cannot find any image of the riches of his grace. It is almost as if everything we have grasped were aimed to make us understand that it is not proportionate to what we have not grasped, just as the God who was visibly made man is for us an open allusion to the God who remained infinite and invisible.

1:8. *Which he has poured out on us superabundantly in all wisdom and insight.*

God has so poured out his grace upon us that he has given us every sort of wisdom and insight, so that we might become capable of grasping that it is he who gives. He has poured out superabundantly not only grace but also all wisdom and insight as well: overlapping our wisdom with his wisdom, our insight with his insight, so that through his wisdom and insight we might be equipped to receive the riches of his grace. On the other hand, moreover, so that we might be capable of receiving his wisdom and insight, he fitted us out from the very beginning with a certain wisdom and insight, which are essentially receptive, vessels for the gift of his wisdom and insight, a natural foundation whose chief function remains to open us up, to make us able to take in and contain, to give us the necessary holding capacity. He deposits something in us so that he can put in even more. And after he has made the first deposit, he expects it to expand within us to a unity that expresses the longing to grow into his unity, to place ourselves at the service of his greater wisdom. No one who believes may ever consider his gifts—which, in fact, all derive from God—as his personal property; he must acknowledge and possess them in the willing determination to keep them ready for divine grace; nor is this grace simply the outpouring of wisdom and insight; rather, it is the grace of mission as such. Just as previously loving and being loved were one, so now the inchoate human wisdom and insight bestowed by God and the corresponding infinite wisdom and insight of God himself are in unity. This relationship is the ultimate ground of the superabundance of the outpouring.

The wisdom and insight that are poured out in us are a participation in God's wisdom and insight; he must give us these things if we are supposed to be capable of accepting his teaching and his demands in an increasing measure. *Wisdom* in this regard is more that which brings about man's obedience and his remaining at attention even when he does not understand. *Insight* means rather the attempt to penetrate into the mysteries according to God's bidding. The former is more an attitude, the latter is more an act. The former is abiding within the compass of God's enveloping presence. The latter is striving to find points of contact, to accommodate and enlarge oneself.

1:9. *Making known to us the mystery of his will, according to his gracious design, which he preordained in himself.*

God lets us know the mystery of his will, though he does not reveal it to us all at once but lets us grow into the mystery. Like the way he makes us come to be in the Son. For if he definitively revealed to us his mystery, we would also be able to and would have to distinguish within his will the limits and contours of our existence, of our destiny and also of our surrender; we would survey ourselves from above, and, as a result, faith, hope, and love in trusting self-surrender would be rendered impossible. But God lets us know only that he intends us to understand his will more and more so that we might place our will within his will. We have to desire knowledge, not of what he does not wish to reveal to us, but rather of that mystery of his will that he has purposed to disclose; this mystery, moreover, is in no way exhausted by what he expects of us as individuals but leads beyond that into the mysteries of his universal salvific will. It is not our individual destiny that God wishes to unveil but rather the essence of his will in general. In fact, a man learns obedience better, not if his superior explains to him with more and more detail his duty in particular, but by grasping in an attitude of listening obedience what it means to command in general. The believer, therefore, in obeying the will of God, will grow beyond the particular association of this command and this execution into a sense of the ways and the will and the decree of God in the world in general. He will learn to understand even what is not his own reality, even other ways in which

God's will is realized. If, for example, this will requires renunciation of him, he will also understand it when it means enjoyment for another. Knowing God's will for the consecrated state, he will without a doubt be able to understand his will for the married state. Otherwise, in fact, the knowledge of the divine will would always be referred and limited to one's own ego, and man would be increasingly tempted to question indiscreetly God's ways with him, which in the end would make every obedience impossible. On this account, insight into the divine will must extend itself horizontally, must try to make itself adequate to the dimensions of the divine.

God's will is *mystery* and remains so as well. God introduces us into this mystery, but not in such a way that it simply stops being mysterious. It cannot be exhausted by being revealed; just as in God the unveiling of a part of his being is always the opening of unlimited horizons in other directions, and at the same time to be drawn into God's mystery is a secret of intimacy. At the very moment when lovers are together, they do not interrogate and sound each other out but are—much more so, for example, than when they are reunited after a separation —content with being at one, though this is something they do not discuss and may not even understand. Lovers who pray together or contemplate in common something pertaining to God will not pry out of each other afterward what they have experienced in their prayer; perhaps they will spontaneously tell each other this or that, but they will not feel the lack of what has not been talked about. Lovers will not themselves establish the limits of what is to be confided, of what as lovers they would be entitled to lay claim to: they will always leave these limits to the other. It is the same in the knowledge of God's will. Every aspect of God's mystery that he gives us to understand is surrounded by mystery and opens into greater mystery.

We come to know the mystery of God's will in his Son, in us, and in the Church. Paul has learned it by dint of a powerful personal experience, in his conversion and mission and in his life of faith. But this place of experiential learning in his case is only the point of departure for knowing God's will in the Son, who converted and sent him, and in the Church, in which he has to work.

We do not come to know the will of God by chance but *according to his gracious design*. His design is his loving will to introduce us into his loving will. This will is thus a source and a destination at the same time, and this identity of the beginning and the end is in turn his gracious design itself.

Which he preordained in himself. The design is a part of the mystery of God's will: the part that he reveals to us but that cannot be separated from the whole of the eternal will and is therefore suited at the same time to convey some sense of the infinity of the mystery hidden in the whole of God's will. God forms this design *in himself*, in a divine freedom that has no need of any creature in order to make plans and to carry them out at the time he has appointed. He avails himself of creatures within his design only insofar as they may be necessary to make known its force and validity. He *preordains* this design in the priority of his triune life with respect to the created universe, and once it has been made he inserts the creation and its entire meaning into this preexisting design. And this design is a *gracious one*, for God knows no other kind of designs for men than those he ordains in relation to his Son, namely, goodness, love, and grace.

1:10. *To this end: to bring to maturity the fullness of time and to recapitulate all things in Christ as the head, things in heaven and things on earth, in him.*

Unless God makes use of extraordinary means to communicate his will to a man directly, we normally always learn of his plans only after they are fulfilled, when we can look back on them as something that, relatively speaking, has been brought to conclusion. So it is a general rule that we must always let time proceed toward its full maturity in order to understand God's design. The great conclusion, however, that casts light upon everything is the Son. But the Son's visible manifestation on earth is in itself only a beginning, an opening, from which it becomes possible for us, as we continue our journey and our striving together with the Son, to grow into the ever greater plenitude of the mysteries of God. The Lord's years on earth were for us the portal through which we were initiated into the central mystery of the love between Father and Son. For wherever something of this mystery disclosed itself, it was revealed that in that mystery the Son was in communion with us, both as the Incarnate One, through whose humanity we had won access to the divine, and as the Son of God, who graciously wished to let us participate in his sonship. We were thus able to recognize in faith during the time of his visibility that he was ceaselessly exchanging love and being with the Father, that his whole being was explicable only in terms of this exchange. Because this exchange revealed itself to be supernatural, we cannot suppose that it was restricted to the time of the Son's life on earth; we know that through his visibility we have received a share in the mysteries of eternity and that what the Son—by way of recapitulation —represented to us of the plan and design of the Father during his time on earth was ultimately only a representation of what is played out from everlasting to everlasting between Father and Son in heaven and into which God wills to draw us through the creation and through the Incarnation of the Son.

The mystery of which Paul speaks here and which he lays open, therefore, is by no means the quintessence of all God's mysteries, as if whoever had understood this mystery (supposing it were fully comprehensible) thereby possessed a sort of key to all God's mysteries and acquired a kind of overview of God. Rather, in the fullness of time, the Son opens a view into the unfathomable depths of the mystery of God, which is the mystery between the Father and the Son in the Holy Spirit; and everything in the world that hitherto seemed perspicuous is now referred to this mystery, becomes a function of this mystery, can no longer be interpreted except in the light of this never-to-be-fathomed mystery. For what is laid open in the Son is that the Father has decided to *recapitulate all things in heaven and on earth* in this Son, this Son whose divinity and humanity withdraw him from every univocal master vision and whose relationship to the Father gives him full title to be the eternally Mysterious One. That all things

are to have their part in this Son means that they all are
to be caught up into his mystery.

For this reason, even the process of recapitulation itself
remains a mystery. It is impossible to imagine it. We know
only in faith that it takes place and that it is a mystery of
the love of the Father for the Son, of a love in which we
are all to have a share. Only beginnings of this recapitulation were revealed to us in the earthly life of the Lord,
in order to give us a chance to expand our insight. We
learned that the Son was promised in the Old Testament,
and it thus became clear that the Old Testament would
have to pass into him, that the Son would be the recapitulation of the Old Covenant. And since the Messiah was
prophesied as the fulfillment of the Old Covenant, which
was a covenant with the people, a social covenant, it was
equally clear that the New Covenant, the Church, was to
find herself in an intimate unity with the Messiah, that
Christ was also to be the recapitulation of the Church.
And we furthermore learned that when the Son shed his
blood on the Cross to redeem us, he took our sins upon
himself and there recapitulated all our sins in himself in
order to blot them out. It follows that in the Son there are
many recapitulations ascertainable in his earthly manifestation. But Paul now informs us that we must conceive
of these apparently limited recapitulations as having been
expanded to the unlimited plan of the Father: to recapitulate everything in heaven and on earth in the Son and,
in him, the head, to renew it.

For that which is recapitulated in the Son, who is God,
cannot remain without being in itself transformed. By
assuming the form of the Eucharist, the Son transforms

himself into a new state, but he also transforms us, into whom he enters eucharistically. He draws us into his Eucharist. At first he transforms as if from the inside out, by letting himself become eucharistic, by shifting his center into the host. But because he can do that, he can also do the opposite: transform from the outside in, drawing things into his center. And since the Father is aware of this power, he can plan the transformation of all things into the Son and their recapitulation in him. The Father places all things into the Son's hands as a sort of "food" for him and for his mission: he assimilates things to him, but in such a way that he lets the Son become a food for the world eucharistically. Naturally, things do not become transformed into Christ himself, they do not disappear like the bread and wine in the consecration. But they find in the Son their fulfillment, the place where they can be themselves; the Son leads all things to what they are meant to be in God's design by impressing upon them his stamp and character.

This consignment of all things to the Son does not simply coincide with the redemption, for even heavenly things, which do not have need of the redemption, are consigned to him, and even earthly things can already be good. The redemption is only a part, a phase within this overall plan of the Father for things. The Father commits them all to the Son's charge so that he may bring them back to the Father as things of the Son. In this recapitulation, even the distinctions between heaven and earth are relativized, inasmuch as now the only absolute property of things is: to be in Christ. In light of that, the distance between heaven and earth has become insignificant.

The transformation things undergo by entering into Christ's possession could be compared to the transformation of an ordinary object, a piece of cloth, for example, into a relic by virtue of having been carried by someone like a saint. Looked at from the outside, the piece of cloth has not altered. But its inner worth and content have become entirely different. Before it was a worthless rag, now it is a precious treasure. In the same way things become infinitely valuable and dear to the Father because Christ touches them—as he does through the Incarnation and the Eucharist. This transformation is a quality that is given to things by the hands of love. For that reason it is not merely exterior, in the sense of a juridical property right of the Son over things; it is not a rigid title that simply closes up a deal. It is something living and life-giving that, as such, leads farther and opens. The Father recapitulates in the Son only in order to be able to move ahead with much more ease, in order to design more and more fluidly and copiously the opening from himself to the world and from the world to himself in the Son. Thanks to this recapitulation in the Son, all things are possible gifts. The Son transforms things in such a way that they become meaningful and profitable within love. Just as in the carnal relation between man and woman everything is there in order to be transformed into something spiritual and spiritually fruitful and, in this transformation, to acquire entirely new significances.

1:11. *In whom we were also chosen to be heirs, having been predestined according to the purpose of him who works all things according to the counsel of his will.*

Without him we would have no rights of inheritance. But in him we have every such right. For in him we become those whom God calls his children. At the creation, God the Father had made Adam his son; but through sin Adam fell out of the grace of filiation and thus forfeited his filial rights. But by allowing us in the Son to become partakers of the right of inheritance a second time, God gives us a security Adam did not have: the security of no longer being able to incur the loss of the inheritance. By virtue of the Incarnation it was as though a new law of inheritance were created for men, for from now on the Son is the full realization of man, and he brings from heaven the law of his son- and heirship, in which he entitles as coheirs the others who are his brothers. Since the Father plans to recapitulate everything in him, he has entrusted them to the Son so that they have no choice but to become an enduring testimony to this new filiation. The Son will never cease to be the child of God, any more than he will cease to have become man for us, which is to assure us of participation in his heavenly law of inheritance. We have accordingly become *heirs* in him, and have become so because we *were predestined* for this *according to the purpose of* the Father. The Father knew that it would be necessary to draw us into the Son's law of inheritance so that we would no longer be able to fall from the filial state. And the Father who conceived this purpose is the one who *works all things*; nothing is done according to his intention that has not been worked by him personally. This is what the Son shows us, the Son who knows no other will than that of the Father, who in the name of the Father works everything the Father works in his own will and who consequently invites us through the law of filiation that he introduces to live according to the Father's determination and to let everything we work have its effect through God. And he works everything *according to the counsel of his will*. The will of the Father is the will that determines everything, so that everything that is recapitulated in the Son and concerns our filiation and entitlement as heirs has its place within this preordained purpose.

1:12. *So that we, who hoped in Christ before, might be a praise of his glory.*

That we are to be a *praise of the glory* of God means in truth that each of us has to fulfill the mission of the Son. The Son came to glorify the Father, and we come into the world to praise this glorification. In this praise, our glorification of God and the Son's glorification of God are recapitulated, and the second is the enabling condition of the first. It is only through the Son that we know how to glorify the Father. And since we are not the Son and cannot glorify the Father in the way the Son does, we can become a praise of the glorification, namely, of the Son, who is the recapitulation of all glorification of the Father. Of course, we too attempt to glorify the Father, but, since we hardly know how, we praise the perfect way in which the Son glorifies him, which is without a doubt the correct way. We do this in much the same way we ask a saint to support our requests with God; although we also try to pray ourselves, we have confidence that the saint knows better how to pray appropriately and that he brings our prayer in the right way before God.

Who hoped in Christ beforehand. Here Paul speaks primarily in the name of the Jews, who believed in the promise. But beyond that there is also a possibility for others to be introduced into faith through hope in Christ. Paul has in mind here both at once: the Jews, who believed in the promise and thus hoped in the Messiah and who can join in the praise of the glorification now that this promise has been fulfilled in the new faith in Christ—and then those individuals who allowed themselves to be seized and guided by a personal hope and by this route attained to faith and love.

Hope in the Lord has a particular character. It is not simply a vague expectation of better conditions. It is something that is opened up supernaturally because the Lord already lives in this hope, because anyone who shares this sort of hope already participates in a hidden way in the Lord's hope. At its point of origin in the Lord, this hope is one with faith and love, but in this particular one who hopes the character of hope impresses first. Furthermore, this hope contains from the very outset a sort of surrender. Where this anticipatory hope begins to take shape, the one who hopes foregoes the right to test and to direct everything to come. He is ready in advance to meet what comes with surrender. When fulfillment arrives, he will not say that it is other than he expected. In this openness lies the Christian character of anticipatory hope, which necessarily contains something of the character of faith and love; for between the three reigns a sort of reciprocal inhabitation. This hope is anchored in the Lord to such a degree that it has nothing in common with purely earthly hopes, which can be disappointed; for example, a sick man's hope for recovery, a hope entirely centered in man. Hope in the Lord has its center in the Lord, it is a movement that tends away from the ego, that rises toward God, that shifts its center of gravity to God. There are certain human grades in between: one can selflessly hope good things for a fellow man, and because Christ has become man and because he lives in every neighbor, such a hope can already bear a germ of supernatural hope.

We have to hope in Christ *in advance*, in the same way that we generally have to do many things in advance, because all of Christ's deeds were performed in advance, in eternity, in God's eternal design. Christian life lives by this anticipation: thus, the Yes spoken at the child's baptism, for example, determines his life in advance; when he later repeats this Yes personally and consciously, he is granted no other starting point. The Yes of the convert who approaches the Church without yet being able to subscribe to everything because he does not yet know it, has not yet learned it, is once again a Yes in advance. It is the same with the Yes to the married state or to the consecrated state: he who binds himself to it by no means has a panoramic view of what he is obliging himself to, of what consequences his assent can have. And so it is in every obedience.

1:13. *After having heard the word of truth, the gospel of your salvation, you too believed in him and were sealed with the Holy Spirit of the promise.*

You too: This is the way Paul suddenly addresses the receivers of the letter. They are Gentiles, in contrast to the Jews among whom Paul previously reckoned himself. As "you", they are at the same time those who are to be drawn into the "we" of the Church, of the communion of faith in whose name Paul addresses them. Of course, they are themselves already Christians and belong to the Church. But it is as if the Apostle wanted to reopen to discussion of their relation to faith, to describe from scratch the fact of their incorporation as members. The foregoing could have given them the impression that Paul had spoken about certain mysteries of God, Christ, and man on a theological plane, which perhaps appeared too difficult to lay any serious obligation on them. Now, however, Paul addresses them directly and plunges them into the midst of the mystery: *you too!* These mysteries of God's will, of existence in the Son, concern them urgently and personally. He has told them these things only because they are so deeply concerned in them. For they, too, *believed* and did so after they *heard the word of truth*, which is not just any gospel, any message, but the *gospel* of their *salvation*.

Those who believe have heard the word of truth from the Lord. And he himself is the *Word of truth*. Outside of his word there is no truth, because every truth is comprised in it. Outside of his word there is not even a word, because he himself is the Word. And this word of truth is *the gospel of salvation*, because the message of the Lord explains his mission, and he was sent by the Father to accomplish man's salvation. Everyone who hears the word belongs to those for whom the gospel was proclaimed, so that when he hears the word of truth he has to believe in it. As soon as those who hear know that the word of the Lord is the truth and that the Lord is the Word, this knowledge immediately becomes faith, and this faith is no longer separable from the message of their salvation.

Because they believed, they *were sealed with the Holy Spirit*. The Spirit marks them with his signature. They thus know: they have been sealed by the Spirit in the Son according to the design of the Father in the Son. The Spirit mediates to them the Father's will to see them in the Son. Faith, whose obligation reaches down to their innermost self and on that account leads them to the point where the Father wants to have them: *in him,* namely, in the Son. They remain there in virtue of the seal imparted by the Holy Spirit, who gives them stability. He is the Spirit of *the promise*. He is indivisibly linked to the promise of the Son. Son and Spirit are contained within the same promise, just as God himself, who pronounced this promise, cannot be divorced from this promise. By this means it is revealed that the triune God in each of his three Persons has an active part in the faith of Christians, not only insofar as he communicates the bare gift of faith, but also insofar as he determines the position, the surrender, the mission, the whole Christian life of the believer. The Father, who carries out his eternal purpose with regard to the predestination of men, does so in unity with the Son and the Spirit; he allots the Son the task of

assuming man into himself, and to the Spirit he assigns
the charge of offering surety that man will remain in the
Lord. The *sealing* by the Holy Spirit is this guarantee of
staying power, this establishing of man's permanent place,
this steadying and fixing. He is at the same time a witness,
as he was a witness of the Father's working of the Son's
Incarnation in the Mother, witness to the Father that his
will has been fulfilled and that we are in the Son. He confirms. And this confirmation is not merely external but is
given through a wholly interior mark and corroboration;
it is a seal. A seal that is just as much in Christians as
in God; like a rope that is slung around man but in like
manner around God, so that if man tried to free himself
on his side from this bond, he would still not succeed in
dissolving the bond fastened to God. In God it continues
to exist and does so forever and is not affected by man's
attempts to get loose. That is the indelibility of the impress of the Spirit.

1:14. *Who is the pledge of our inheritance in view of the redemption of those who were acquired, to the praise of his glory.*

The Spirit is a pledge of our inheritance, a pledge God
the Father gives us in the Son. We cannot be in the Son
in any other way than as sealed by the Spirit, bearing the
impressed mark of the Spirit. With this sign we can certify
before God that we are his, that we have been adopted
by him, that we have the right to his inheritance. But
the pledge is not just on one side; it obliges us to accept
the inheritance of the Father and to remain in the Son. If
God the Father has given us the pledge of his inheritance

through the seal of the Holy Spirit, we can no longer erase the seal of this pledge that we have stipulated; we remain those who have been marked before God and stand in a relationship to his inheritance, whose terms have already been arranged. We remain before him the party who has accepted, just as before us he remains the party who has accepted us. And we are accepted in view of *the redemption of those* whom God has acquired. There is a community in view of the redemption. We are not alone as redeemed men; we belong to the host of those whom God has *acquired* for himself. The mark of the Holy Spirit suddenly becomes one that no longer forms merely the relationship of the individual to God and of God to the individual, but ex-presses the communion of those who have been sealed in the Holy Spirit. The salvation of each one of us hangs together with the salvation of everyone else. In view of this salvation of the one and common inheritance of God's, we have been *acquired* by God. God the Father himself, by having the Son become man for the redemption of men, constituted the communion of all who are to be redeemed by the Son. And he places this whole community into the *praise of his glory*; he lets it share in the mission of the Son, who came to glorify the Father.

1:15–16. *I too, having heard of your faith in the Lord Jesus and of your love toward all the saints, therefore do not cease saying thanks for you, remembering you in my prayer.*

Paul appears here as one who belongs absolutely on the side of God, not only insofar as he believes in God, but also insofar as the meaning of his life consists in working in the name of God. Believers have to know of Paul's mission and of his execution of this mission. It is necessary because Paul, after having spoken of the witness of the Holy Spirit on behalf of the community he is addressing, proceeds to render it a testimony of his own. He has heard of its *faith in the Lord Jesus*, and this hearing obliges him. His obligation was already clear when he began to write and communicate wisdom and insight. It once again becomes clear in a new way when he depicts for them what he does on their behalf because of this hearing. But before that he explains to them what he thinks of them: that he has heard of their faithfulness— which is not merely intellectual but living faith—toward the Lord. Hence he feels himself connected to them on account of this faith. Their faith also appears to him as right and proven because it has generated *love toward all the saints*, that is, because it proves itself to be a true faith by the observance of the Lord's commandment. They live in a unity of faith and love; and if faith seems at first sight to be concerned with the Lord—just as Paul, too, seems to be connected to the Lord by faith—while love appears to have to do with one's fellow men, as if the community thereby responded to the Lord in two different directions, ultimately this is not so, because both faith and love are one: by believing, the community loves the Lord and keeps his commandment, which in turn strengthens it in faith.

Paul had previously spoken of the communion that is formed in the Son by the Spirit according to the Father's design. It was not evident where this communion existed, whether in heaven, in God's design, or on earth; in any case it remained for the time being only on the level of Paul's knowledge. It now emerges that this communion really exists on earth, and exists also in the community Paul is addressing, a community that is a sort of earthly mirror image of the communion of saints in God and which by its faith lives in God also on earth.

John sees the heavenly communion of the saints, as it were, through the earthly one. He customarily begins entirely in the sphere of the senses, in sight, hearing, and touch, in order to extend this experience into the heavenly dimension. Paul, who is much more intellectual, knows of God's plan, of the presence of a heavenly community, and one cannot say that he beholds it in the community on earth; for him vision would first begin where the heavenly reality had become perfectly visible in the earthly. In contrast to John, he begins with the heavenly, in order then to wait and see how much of the earthly can be projected into the heavenly. This approach corresponds to his spiritual make-up. John possesses a certain sensuousness that Paul does not have; he thinks and believes with the whole apparatus of his senses. Paul is more of a thinker; he makes sharp distinctions and is capable of reflecting about everything he does. He is able to back up a step and consider what he has done. John would not be capable of doing that; he is much too intensely involved to be able to get any distance. At the end of his life he would be able to express little about his work, which he feels to be entirely in embryo. Paul, on the other hand, could describe it exactly according to its various stages: he is constantly bringing things to conclusion.

Therefore I do not cease saying thanks for you. He says thanks in a twofold way: he says thanks in their name that God has converted them, that they have been associated with his saints. But he also says thanks in his own name, for their sakes, that in his work he can count on them. That they have been placed in his, the apostle's, path so that he can carry out his work in them: can deepen their faith, expand their knowledge, and so speed them on their way to an independent continuation of the Pauline work. Paul's most essential apostolate consists less in laying the first foundations than in advancing those who are already converted, enlivening existing faith, communicating deeper knowledge of the Christian reality, and therefore equipping believers for the demanding apostolate. His attention was drawn to the community precisely because he had heard of their already existing faith and love.

Remembering you in my prayer. In this prayer, then, he speaks with God and discusses his apostolate with him. We thus get a glimpse of the double form of his apostolic activity. One form is more active: he instructs, he announces what was made known to him. The other is more contemplative: he prays and knows that his prayer is heard. He also knows that the prayer of the saints is an expression of their communion and that through his prayer for the community he strengthens its communion. They must also know that he prays for them so that they may feel strengthened. But knowing that he does so, they must also learn how necessary prayer is.

1:17. *So that the God of our Lord Jesus Christ, the Father of glory, may give you the spirit of wisdom and of revelation in the knowledge of him.*

Paul asks God for the spirit of wisdom on the community's behalf. This prayer will be granted for two reasons: first, because the spirit of wisdom is the content of the prayer; second, simply because Paul prays, and his prayer, even when not formulated expressly, can yield nothing other than the spirit of wisdom. The community, which through its faith and love has been drawn into the sphere of his mission, will necessarily receive a share in the special grace of the Apostle's mission, which consists in mediating God's wisdom.

He mediates, but the one who gives is *the God of our Lord Jesus Christ*. Paul describes him now, not as the Father, but as God, as the one toward whom our Lord, the man Jesus Christ, stood in a relationship of obedience similar to that in which a believer stands vis-à-vis God. And because the community lives according to the Lord's command and believes in him, it will desire nothing other than to believe in the one who for their Lord Jesus Christ is God. He who believes in the Lord believes also in his God. The Lord, too, since he was a genuine man and the first Christian, had a human relationship to the triune God. What he transmits to us as the content of faith was also the content of his human consciousness, even though the act in which he possessed this content was infinitely perfect and included in the vision of the Father as an act of obedience. But he possessed the power to veil even this vision from himself—on the Cross, for example—in order to emphasize that obedience which he will bestow on us in the act of faith. He utters the cry: "My God, why have you forsaken me?" in the greatest proximity to the believing man, after he has veiled the divine side of the vision in himself. The Lord's ability to be wholly man is very clear to Paul; and man cannot live from knowledge alone, he must believe, and this means to participate in the Lord's perfect act of self-surrender to his God.

The Father of glory. The God of the Lord, who is also the God of believers, now appears as the Father of glory, because both the Lord and believers belong to this glory. On the one hand, he is the Father of glory as the Father of the Son and of believers, who give him this glory, and, on the other hand, as the one who has himself generated every glory.

So that he may give you the spirit of wisdom and of revelation in the knowledge of him. This spirit also belongs to the glory of the Father. For the Father eternally possesses the whole of wisdom and revelation with himself. But he wishes to give it. The Son is the revelation of the wisdom of the Father, whereas the Holy Spirit is the one who communicates both the wisdom and the revelation. God cannot give this spirit otherwise than *in the knowledge of him.* God bestows the knowledge of God upon the community; and God the Father is contained in this knowledge in the form of wisdom, God the Son in the form of revelation and God the Holy Spirit in the form of the communication of wisdom and revelation, so that now the Father seems to possess, as it were, a predominance, since he contains the whole life of the Trinity in himself, and the knowledge of the Spirit and of the Son leads finally to the knowledge of the Father.

On the other hand, Paul must utter precisely this prayer. For if all have to prayer for the fulfillment of God's will, everyone must nonetheless ask within his particular mission. But Paul knows that wisdom, revelation, and knowledge constitute in particular the content of his mission. Hence for him it is the same thing to ask for the fulfillment of God's will, for the fulfillment of his mission, or for wisdom and revelation in the knowledge of God for the community.

1:18. *So that he may enlighten the eyes of your heart, to make you understand what is the hope of his calling, what are the riches of the glory of his inheritance among the saints.*

That also the eyes of their hearts might be enlightened, this is now the content of Paul's prayer. If before he had requested above all wisdom, revelation, and knowledge for them, he now requests the light of the heart, so that their gift of themselves may not remain an affair of the understanding alone but may become a matter of heartfelt love. They are not only to concern themselves with God in moments of deepened insight but must feel themselves seized by God in their innermost being, in their heart, so that everything they do and hope for may remain in an enduring harmony with their love for God. They are to feel themselves bound to God right through their heart. If the eyes of their heart are enlightened, they will walk in the light of the triune God; the possibility of betaking themselves into the shadows, of withdrawing from the radiance of his grace, will have been taken away from them. The grace Paul implores for them is, consequently, Pauline through and through: he wishes for them an abiding self-surrender, joined with an enduring light. He is not thinking now of the night of the cross that can sink down upon a soul. He is, as it were, in a sort of convert's mood, and his whole life long he can think of nothing lovelier. He sees life entirely in the perspective of the return to the Father. And if he suspected that the cross, in the sense of the interior night, stood before a Christian, he would be of the opinion that he himself, the apostle, must take this night upon himself so that this Christian could carry on in the community enlightened from within. That the night of the soul can be the most fruitful thing in a Christian's life, that one would impoverish a life by removing the night from it, Paul has not yet had any opportunity to think of that. He lives in the first generation; he has no way of generalizing his own experiences. Only the experience of the Church will allow the thought to occur that even the experiences of the apostles exist to be transmitted.

To make you understand what is the hope of his calling. In the first place, it must be understood that God calls, that the one called must answer, that this call carries with it a hope, which is fulfilled when, in answering, man has apprehended this hope. In the second place, it must be understood that the more peremptory, the more abrupt the call, the greater is the hope. Calls are graduated. If someone answers a greater call, he can thereby make hope light up in all vocations, and he can ignite many other hopes with his answer.

What are the riches of the glory of his inheritance among the saints. One can grasp the riches of the glory of God only from an enlightened heart; the naked intellect is not sufficient to penetrate to the core of love. And these riches of God are manifested in his saints, in the inheritance with which he endows them, because he gives to his saints from the store of his own most personal property. He gives them things beyond the conception of unbelievers, because such things can be grasped by the eyes of faith alone. He makes them his children and bestows upon them his inheritance: the very glory of the Father that the Son had come to announce. And at the moment when the Son was praising him, the Father bestowed it upon him in a new fashion by granting it to his saints. Just as the will of the Son was that the Father recognize him in those who believe, so now the Father wills that, through the bestowal of glory on believers, the Son may find the glory of the Father reflected in them. Accordingly, the saints are doubly tied to heaven: by the Son, who redeems them, and by the Father, who bestows upon them his glory. The whole of this is the inheritance, the participation in everything that is the Father's: the Father himself and the Son in their unity in the Spirit.

1:19. *And what is the exceeding greatness of his power toward us who believe, as it is revealed in the working of the power of his might.*

This power is exceedingly great because it extends without limit over everything that is God's, in heaven and on earth. Only in faith can we form some idea of the power of God. The nonbeliever who tried to form an idea of God would restrict his power; he would have to start from the limited compass of what can be known to men and on that basis attempt to construct God's power. The believer, on the other hand, knows that the entire world that can be grasped and thought is but a minuscule fragment of what God can do; in order to gauge God's power, the believer does not begin with the world but immediately with God. As faith grows, what we know or guess of God, and, therefore, the real intimation that his power is ever exceedingly greater, simultaneously expands. The barriers of our intellect and of our conceptual apparatus cease to count, and God can deploy his entire power in our faith, even if we are quite far from totally comprehending it. Faith gives God back, as it were, his entire power. This is why Paul emphasizes the power of God *toward us who believe*.

As it is revealed in the working of the power of his might. It manifests itself in its working as a sign of its presence. But even at the point where it becomes visible in its operation, the dimensions of its greatness can be guessed at only in faith. The connections between the event and the cause, which lies in the power of God itself, can, in turn, be grasped only by faith. The intellect without faith would seek other connections and would never arrive at the truth. For if God is the truth, and the Son is the revelation of this truth, then faith is the key that allows us to draw near to this revelation. We understand the power of God's might in its being as well as in its revelation in action only through the gift of faith bestowed upon us by God.

1:20. *Which he wrought in Christ by raising him from the dead and setting him at his right hand in the heavenly places.*

In order to display the power of the Father, Paul refers to two examples from the life of the Son: his Resurrection and his Ascension. It is here, in his opinion, that the power of the Father has revealed itself most radiatingly. But in order to understand that Christ has risen from the dead and ascended into heaven and that the Father has performed these actions, one needs faith. Unbelief will never acknowledge either the Resurrection and Ascension of the Son or the sign of the Father's power. Faith can. Even the hesitant faith of Thomas was, at the moment it recognized the Son of God in the Risen One, convinced of the Father's power. Faith goes farther. It acknowledges even that which the Son merely promised, that of which faith itself no longer has an accompanying experience, that for which it possesses no further possibilities of proof except in faith in the Son: the reception into heaven, the sitting at the right hand of the Father. And yet it is the same faith, laden with the same properties, that acknowledges the one as well as the other. He who believes in the Resurrection believes neither more nor less than he who believes in the sitting at the right hand of God. The two demonstrations of power are a unity, and this unity is situated both in the will of the Father and in the faith of the one who believes in the God, Father, Son, and Holy Spirit. By means of those demonstrations of power, God not only created this unity but at the same time proved it. And Paul lends both demonstrations the characteristic of the Father's infinite power. They prove that God the Father is not bound to the worldly laws that he himself invented but can blast them open at any moment, can replace earthly laws with heavenly ones. At the same time, they prove that he is lord of all in heaven, that he himself confers the place at his right and fills it with the Son. He carries things through that a priori appeared impossible. If he does not perform them unexpectedly, but after he has promised them, this is only so that, since we have expected them, we can better understand them as wonders and demonstrations of power when they are carried out and can abide in faith from the expectation to the fulfilling of it. As Christians we already believed in advance, but our hope and our faith have not been disappointed. God has fulfilled and thereby shown that his power lies not only in the mere execution but in the filling up and disposition of the times, in the extension throughout history of his power to accomplish.

It is the Father who raises the Son on Easter and exalts him in the Ascension; the Son lets the end of the work of redemption issue in a triumphal celebration of the Father; He overcomes death in order to let the perfect power of the Father attain its consummated representation in him, the Son. He leaves the work of the Resurrection to the Father, even though he, who, after all, is God, could have raised himself. He does not do it actively, just as he did not place himself in Mary's womb.

1:21. *Far above every dominion and authority and power and dignity and every name that can be named not only in this age but also in the age to come.*

Paul continues to describe the display of the Father's power in the Son, always with the intention of familiarizing the community with the glory of God, to whose praise it is called through participation in the heavenly inheritance. The Father set the Son far above every dominion, authority, power, and dignity and thus showed plainly that none of these authorities can measure up to his power. They are all subject to him by his will. In the world and in the Church there are hierarchies, structures, and organizations that have various grades and thus boast signs of dominion, display power, and confer honors, but all of this remains under the supreme lordship of God; nor is any of it challenged by the supreme lordship of God but, rather, is confirmed by it. It is in no way the case that the fact of the supreme majesty of God calls into question every inner-worldly dominion, authority, power, and dignity or degrades them. It can sanction them, augment them, enlarge their scope; but its own scope remains eternally exalted above the scope of this power held by its sufferance. And every worldly power and hierarchy can be tested for the validity and legitimacy of its existence according to whether the following evidence is furnished in its behalf: it stands under God's power. Under not only in the sense of the lesser but also in that of the truly subordinate, which does not dare enter into any competition with the absolute power.

This power also stands *far above every name that can be*

named not only in this age but in the age to come. In no age
of the world can anything be found that could elude the
prior determination of God. So that here Paul subjects
not only the present order of things to God's power but
also everything to come, the conceivable and the incon-
ceivable, that which can be hinted at and that which cannot, whatever can be named. He thus withdraws from
the creature once and for all the possibility of setting up
as good or perfect or desirable anything that is not en-
compassed by the greater power of God. God's power
surpasses every other, not only in intensity, but also in
temporal extension. No evolution of the world, no "infinite progress" will change anything in the relationship
between the power of God and that of his creatures. For
all eternity God will surpass the most perfect creature by
the infinite measure of his Godhead.

By conferring upon the risen Son his infinite power
and setting him far above every power, God the Father
did not restrict his own power but rather magnified it in
relation to the world. He showed that his love for the
Son is so great that he places everything at his disposition, even what pertains primarily to the Father's own
attributes: his power. Insofar as he truly bestows it upon
the Son, he knows that the Son will use it in the spirit of
his will for his glorification. He will be glorified to the
degree that the power of the Son proves to be stronger
than every worldly power and in that the Son makes every power that he surpasses grow into the power of the
Father. By surpassing every power above which he is exalted, he impresses upon it the characteristics of the Father, for he recapitulates in himself all things in heaven

and on earth by surpassing them. This is a mystery that hangs together with his birth: by becoming man, he, while already in possession of the Father's power, brought the power of the Father into the Mother. The action of the Father's seed in the Mother is a sign that the Son surpasses the laws and the power of the world. He already indicates this superiority by means of the Virgin Birth, but the Mother is marked with it in that she becomes pregnant by God for God. She is equipped with a power that, through her submission to God, elevates her above the powers of the world. From this point, the law works itself out further: in raising Lazarus, the Lord evidences his power over death; Lazarus has the characteristics of this power, as do all who have seen the miracle or have heard about it. All powers that subject themselves to the might of the Son are arranged in an order and reflect his power. When the state, for example, allows itself to be surpassed by the power of Christ, then it is visibly clothed with the attributes of God. Until the appearance of the Lord, worldly power was, so to say, ultimately without valence (and there was and is also the power of the devil, whose scope is conceded to him by God and is an evil power). From the moment the Son appears in the world, all powers and authorities, even that of the state, receive a positive valence well only in the measure that they subject themselves to his overlordship or at least do not immediately resist it.

1:22. *And has subordinated everything under his feet and has established him as the all-transcending head of the Church.*

Hence, there is no longer anything that is not comprehended by the lordship of Christ. The Father has put all things in his charge, but in such a way that he has subordinated them to him. The Son will be able to decide upon the order from now on, but within the Father's wish that it always remain an order of subordination under the Son. As if the Father had given him a supreme norm whose interpretation and application he leaves to his discretion on the condition the rule is always respected.

And has set him as the all-transcending head of the Church. Only now, at the end, the Church is mentioned, for the reason that she is the most important thing. The Son becomes her head, but not within an ascending hierarchy, but as a head that *transcends all things*, including every hierarchy. The discontinuity that separates him from the highest rung of the hierarchy is as great as the distance that separates God and man. Of course, the whole Church is led by the Spirit of the Son, and there is no doubt that she draws her life from him, but she cannot do this except by acknowledging the distance that separates her from her transcendent head. Within this distance she remains the decisive witness of the Incarnation of the Son and the realization of God's design. For:

1:23. *She is his body, the fullness of him who is fulfilled in all through all.*

The Lord exercises dominion over his Church in a way analogous to that in which a man rules over his own body.

He fulfills in her that hierarchical principle that has also been entrusted to the individual man. But if the Lord and his Church are related as spirit and body, then they are one. And since the Lord founded the Church when he sojourned bodily on earth, it is easy to understand that the Church, continuing after him, takes over the functions that the fleshly body of the Lord possessed on earth: to embody his spirit for us, to render it present, to make us aware of it, to communicate it. Now it is the Church that does all this, that shows us and presents the Lord to us. But the substitution of the Church in the place of the fleshly body of Christ is not realized without the intermediate term of the Eucharist. Through it, Christ builds up for himself by means of his fleshly body, which, however, is now freed from the laws of space and time, the more encompassing body of the Church. And it is clear that the Eucharist can exist meaningfully and legitimately only within the Church: bestowed by the Lord upon the Church, bestowed by the Church upon her members for the edification of the body of Christ through the body of Christ. Every celebration of the Eucharist outside of the Church can never be anything but an inner contradiction. There are not two bodies of Christ; the eucharistic body can be preserved—like a leaven—only within his ecclesial body.

The fullness of him who is fulfilled in all through all. If the Lord and the Church are related like Spirit and body, then in this intimate relationship, it is the Lord who in the first place fills up, indeed, fills up everything, and in this way the Church is his fullness. But if she is, then in a certain sense he needs her in order to reveal his fullness, to bring his fulfillment to all, and in this sense he is also filled up by the Church. There is a reciprocal relationship of fullness and fulfillment between the Lord and the Church. If one wanted to emphasize in every case only one side of the relationship while suppressing the other, one would get a completely empty concept of fullness, just as a fullness that could not deploy itself, could not pour itself out, could not fulfill itself, would not be a real fullness at all. Indeed, even the fullness of the Father, in order to be itself, needs the Son to contain it, and for its part the fullness of the Son flows back to the Father. Every fullness, even the divine fullness, is such only as a reciprocal filling up, even though in this relationship one partner is primarily the one who gives and the other the one who primarily responds. Thus, even the fullness between the Lord and the Church can subsist only in a reciprocal filling up of both, even though the Lord, insofar as he is the all-transcending head, is the one who gives infinitely and the Church the one who receives infinitely. When the Church dispenses a sacrament, she dispenses neither something purely her own nor, on the other hand, something belonging exclusively to the Lord, but something that is filled up by both together. If she had no active share in the grace of Christ, which she administers, she would not be the fullness of Christ. She cannot be merely a lifeless channel, an exterior communication of the fullness of the Lord; she herself belongs to his fullness, is contained in the fullness of his grace, and therefore also contains the fullness of Christ in herself. The Father has set the Son over his fullness as the all-transcending head. But the Son, who founded the Church, has this Church as his body and thus takes her fullness into himself, in order to let her be filled up in him. Thus, in the likeness of the body, the other likeness, that of bride and bridegroom, makes its appearance: the bridegroom is over the bride but draws her to himself, in order thereby to fill her up in himself: that he might fill himself up in her by pouring out his entire energy into her.

THE HOMECOMING OF THE GENTILES

2:1–2. And you, who were dead because of your transgressions and sins, in which you formerly walked, according to the course of this world, according to the prince of the power of the air, of the spirit that is now at work in the sons of disobedience.

Paul continues to interpret the concepts of the Lord's Resurrection and Ascension as demonstrations of the Father's power and to apply them to the Church and to the community he is addressing. In order to make the greatness of the divine power clear to his readership, he has adduced the example of Christ; he now proceeds to apply this example to them.

Christ died because of our sins and rose by the power of God as the conqueror of death. Death and resurrection had an earthly and sensible visibility in him. But in this victory he overcame not only bodily but, above all, spiritual death. The visible element of his Passion and death was the access to and, as it were, the sacrament of the invisible and divine event present in it. And the spiritual death he conquered is the one Paul speaks of here: *you were dead because of your transgressions and sins.* Dead of a death that like every death was final, out of which no more life could be hoped for. And yet was not final, because the Lord assumed these transgressions and sins into that guilt for which he willed to die and, consequently, assumed this death into his death, so that by rising he could make sinners rise again with him. Hence, sins lead to the Cross as to the death of the Lord, who embodies our own death and closes it in himself. And as we die in him, so he rises in us, having bestowed upon us on Easter the gift of the confession of sins, the means by which we can associate ourselves to him in the Resurrection. *You were dead*, your death has thus become something of the past because you have risen again with Christ in the re-mission of sins, to which the sinner has made his contri-bution by the avowal of sin, by confession.

In which you formerly walked according to the course of this world. They formerly walked in transgressions and sins, from transgression to transgression, from sin to sin. They did it individually and all together. The community Paul addresses already formed before its conversion a group of men, a sort of communion. But they carried out their sins not only by free decision, they also let themselves be propelled by the drift of the age; they did what others did too. The accepted thing, the thing nearest at hand was to walk in sin, because, thanks to the work of *the prince of the power of the air*, sin was, so to say, in the air. It was like an infection. They followed this prince with-out noticing who he was. Of course, they did not think they were doing good when they sinned; but a concept of sin had not yet formed in them. It is as if they had had no grounds for resistance because their capacity of discernment was not yet developed. The prince of the power of the air is a human representation and descrip-tion of the invisible working of the devil; just as in past times, when pathogenic agents had not yet been discov-

ered, people spoke of miasmas, of "exhalations" of the
earth or air, which supposedly spread epidemics. And the
image is suitable. There is something like a pollution of
the atmosphere by the devil, a process the sinner does not
perceive but to which saints, on the other hand, can be
very sensitive. Many of them managed to withstand the
corrupt air of humanity only with effort; many fainted on
account of the stench of sin. Of the sin of a determinate
man, but also of the sinfulness of a place, of a dwelling, of
a city. The Church has the power to bind the devil of the
air; she can isolate the agent that for the ordinary man is
perceptible only in its effects; on the one hand, she has the
gift of discernment; on the other hand, she has the power
to pin down that elusiveness of the devil's atmosphere, to
constrain him, to condense and concretize his ubiquity.
When the natural man is particularly fine-tuned, he may
possess a sort of preliminary level of this discernment: a
feeling for what is in the air; when it is explicitly developed it can be termed medial. Yet Christian discernment
of the spirits is not a sort of mere intensification of such
a capacity but a gift that comes from above, from God,
and in its fully developed form can be called mystical.
The medial and the mystical, however, have nothing in
common with each other, they are even opposed to each
other in essence, even though it is not out of the question for the two things, natural feeling and the gift of discernment, to meet in a certain middle zone in one man.
However, the medial endowment would never increase
as the gift of discernment developed. The sinner is simply pulled along by the atmospheric devil. He does not
possess the faculty of differentiation, the sensorium for

evil is blunted in him; he is like the man who lives in
closed rooms and no longer notices the bad air. And thus
one will say that an express ethical feeling for good and
evil does not occur even in the non-Christian without a
certain participation in the Christian gift of discernment.
In both forms of perception, however, in the natural and
in the supernatural, it is obvious that God wanted to im-
plant much more delicacy of feeling in human nature than
for the most part it possesses after the fall.

*Of the spirit that is now at work in the sons of disobedi-
ence.* Before now, this spirit worked in one way or another everywhere. Now it has had to retreat but has not
on that account suffered any loss in power. Its method
and the overall result of its working have remained the
same, only it now works in *the sons of disobedience.* It is
as if the sins and transgressions of the new converts had
been concentrated in the sons of disobedience: what was
formerly generally diffused sin, which seemed somehow
comprehensible and excusable because of the polluted air,
has now become declared rebellion against the Lord. The
Lord divided the atmosphere by his coming and to that
extent cleared it up. From this point on, there remains
only the clear alternative: to renounce walking in sin or
to join the rebellion of the sons of disobedience. They are
disobedient because they do not want to open themselves
to the evident truth of the New Covenant. Paul is thinking here of the Jews, but he could also have Gentiles in
mind, provided they have heard the message of the Lord
and, notwithstanding, do not wish to obey it. The spirit at
work in them is actually the spirit against the Spirit. And
the disobedience in discussion here is not the disobedi-

ence of an individual act or moment but that of an enduring inner state. Just as God the Father has adopted Christians, the children of disobedience have been adopted by
the antispirit.

*2:3. Among whom we too all once lived, in the lusts of our
flesh, fulfilling the desires of the flesh and of our thoughts, and
were by nature children of wrath like the rest.*

Paul reckons himself among them: *we all.* The features
distinguishing those who believe from the children of
disobedience were not yet stamped. All, including Paul
and those who now form the community, lived in *the lusts
of the flesh,* just as do the sons of disobedience even now.
They let their life be guided by the flesh, they knew no
resistance against the appetites but carried out *the desires
of the flesh and of thoughts.* These thoughts, aspirations,
and considerations all likewise stemmed from the flesh.
But now they have become sons of God, these things no
longer proceed from the flesh but from the Lord. Formerly, everything in their spirit stood under the compulsion and law of the body, and it was compulsion because they knew no other law. Everything is compulsory
when one has no choice to do anything else. They followed the law of the atmosphere, which was a law of
pleasure, of enjoyment, of the fulfillment of drives; one
satisfied desire begot the next out of itself, and this, in
its turn, begot the next one. *Flesh* must be taken in the
broadest sense; to it belongs everything that is not the
Spirit of Christ. The spirit of the world, which was described previously, also belongs to it and is guided and

formed by the flesh. The spiritual aspect of man had become subject to the spirit of the prince of the power of the air, and again and again it led the human spirit back to the flesh from which it itself originated. And in this way the devil of the atmosphere had maintained a sort of dominion over the human spirit, a dominion that was not dissimilar to that of the Spirit of the Lord: as the Spirit of the Lord leads the human spirit to the Father, in the same way the spirit of the air repeatedly led him to the flesh.

And we were by nature children of wrath, like the rest. We all possess a human nature, which was created in the beginning by God and which he gave us in order to make us capable of receiving from him the grace of the supernatural. Before the fall, our nature was wholly open to the supernatural; the possibilities of intercourse and dialogue with God were essentially different from what they were later. For sin covered in nature precisely that dimension that was its opening toward God. Thus by reason of sin human nature became a nature turned away from God, a nature that had forfeited the opening to the supernatural. Men became *by nature children of wrath.* The wrath of God is the counterpart on God's side of the original nature's concealment by sin. It is not so much being driven out of paradise that is the hardest punishment for sin as being robbed of this paradisaical possibility of contact with God that was included in the first nature.

Now that the redemption has occurred, the believer has to attempt through individual, ever-renewed "acts" to keep the access to God open in himself. Adam had no need of such acts; he *was* open, essentially and as a permanent state; he did not have to conquer any resistance to come to God.

2:4–5. *But God, who is rich in mercy, for the sake of his great love with which he loved us, vivified us together with Christ, even though we were dead owing to transgressions—you have been saved by grace!*

Into the midst of the corrupt and sinful world Paul sets the word *God.* God intervenes where everything was on its way toward death, where everything seemed hopeless, because everyone infected everyone else and dragged them with us into corruption. Here *God, who is rich in mercy,* appears. It requires the incomprehensible riches of his grace to work precisely where pure hopelessness reigned, inasmuch as sin always bore nothing but sin. *For the sake of his great love with which he has loved us,* God *vivified us together with Christ.* His wealth of mercy reveals itself in this love: that he loved us, *even though we were dead owing to transgressions,* and indeed, so far as it lay in us, definitively dead, because we were children of wrath who had fallen into the power of hell. But the great love with which God loved us can be no other than that with which he has loved his Son from all eternity. And for the sake of the love that unites him with the Son, he cannot leave us in death. Otherwise it would be as if he would deprive the Son, who was present at the creation and in whom and for whom he undertook the whole creation, of the joy of the creation and thereby withdraw from the Son something of his paternal love. If the Father left his creatures once and for all in death, at the same place where

their sin is, he would no longer be able to love them.
But in that case the joy of the Son in the creation of the
Father would be spoiled. Therefore the Father must, for
the sake of the love he bears the Son, vivify them *together*
with the Son. Even in regard to sinners, this was the only
way really to save them. If the Father had raised them as
individuals, independently of the Son, they would have
fallen back once again into death; they would not have
been able to understand their new life; they would have
been unable to accept the gift; they would have had nothing to help them cling to grace. At best a sort of back and
forth between sin and forgiveness, wrath and love, would
have arisen, and it would have produced the impression
that the love of the Father is subject to variations. For this
reason the Father shifts the love he has for us entirely into
the Son and lets us participate in the uniqueness and immutability of his love for the Son; he vivified the Son
one time and included us with our many times in this
once of the Son. In order to fall out of this uniqueness, it
would take an abjuration of the Lord in whom we have
been covivified.

You have been saved by grace! This salvation has taken
place in the trinitarian love of Father and Son. And the
grace that is adjudged to the members of the community
—Paul had previously declared his solidarity with them
in sin, now he speaks only of *their* salvation; for the moment his own plays no role—is a triune grace. When the
Father restores sinners to life together with the Son, the
Son and the Spirit are actively involved in this grace: the
Son, by making himself available to be brought back to
life in a communion with sinners; the Spirit, by impress-

ing upon them, in virtue of his being Spirit, the stamp of vivification, the promised seal. And no one has the right to see in his turning away from sin, in the beginning of a new life, any merit of his own but must know that all is grace. And he must see in this grace something that is not only ever greater but also the property of the triune God, who in this grace turns his essence toward him. If they are saved by grace, then they will also behold the triune God by means of grace. For grace is the making visible of the invisible God.

2:6. *Raised us up together with him and made us sit together in the heavens in Christ Jesus.*

That he raised us with him is clear in the light of what was said before; if we have passed from death to life in union with Christ, we understand that this event takes place within his Resurrection. But the Father does not simply deposit us in the world after this Resurrection but rather receives us into heaven together with his Son. Here, too, he does not separate us from the Son. In an infrangible unity with him, we enter the place reserved for him in the heavens. We are, in other words, copartakers of eternal life thanks to our coresurrection. We are no longer shut up in a limited earthly existence but are received together with him into heaven, and even now our soul is allowed a part in the joys of eternal life. We obtain a share in them in a union with the Lord, whose love for the Church and in the Church lives on earth as it does in heaven, so that heaven and earth are bestowed upon us anew in him and the Christian can affirm from now on that in faith—

that means, *in Christ Jesus*—he lives as much in heaven as on earth. The boundaries between the two have tumbled away; they have been removed by the Father in the Son; but because we were in union with the Son, this removal affected us as well. And whatever can concern us in any way from now on does so in this double relation of life on earth and in heaven. In his Incarnation, the Son lived this double existence as our perfect archetype. Not only that, but as something that was not concluded with his Ascension but through all ages comes to be ever anew in him and in us. After his Ascension, he lives up in heaven, but he proceeds to live in us, his body, on earth. And we, his body, live on earth, but in him, our head, we live in heaven.

2:7. *That in the ages to come he might show the overflowing wealth of his grace in his kindness toward us in Christ Jesus.*

In the coming ages of the world, there will always be sinners who do not find the way to the Lord and whom the Father nonetheless loves with the same love as he loves those who are already converted and as he loves the Son. It is all these to whom the Lord, in order to counter the prince of the power of the air, wishes to show the abundance of his grace. The men who are to come must not think that God's grace diminishes, that they are no longer as graced as those who lived as contemporaries of the Lord or immediately after him. God wishes to have mercy on them, not in a hidden or inaccessible way, but by disclosing to them the proofs of his grace just as generously as he did to the first Christians. The whole of his

grace, however, will always consist in that act of vivify-
ing together with Christ; here lies the visible evidence *of
his goodness toward us in Christ Jesus* and *of the wealth of his
grace*. It is the Lord in whom the Father gathers together
his whole love and kindness; in him we catch sight of his
grace. In the visible Son the Father becomes present to
us. And because the Father remains turned to us permanently and irrevocably in the Son, his grace confers upon
the Incarnation of the Son and his earthly existence a duration and continuity in which all acts and occurrences
preserve the force of something contemporary that is always happening at this very moment. Even though the
Son died in his body on the Cross once and was raised
once, this unique event, together with everything that
made up his life, was endowed with the nature and the
vigor of something that endures perennially. No episode
from his history has any other meaning than to prove
to us that it is right here that we encounter the Father's
kindness toward us in the Son. This kindness reveals an
overflowing wealth of grace, because there is nothing in the
Son that is closed in itself; rather, everything tends into
the infinity and superabundance of the Father and always
reveals the whole of his grace. Even what seems to us to
be in some sense trifling and incidental in him is immense
and final, because it is included in the Father and because
only on account of our incomprehension does the Son
show it to us in such a way that we can catch at least a
few rays of it.

2:8. *For by grace you have been saved through faith, nor is this of yourselves; it is God's gift.*

With this *for*, Paul sums up the last verse in order to give renewed emphasis to the fact that it is grace that accomplishes the work of redemption. The grace that from all eternity lived in the Father and became visible in the Son. The Son and grace form a unity, the incarnate Son is the expression of the grace of the whole Trinity for the world: of his grace as well as that of the Father and of the Spirit. Of the Father we know that from all eternity it was his intention to save men through the Son, for this salvation was an aspect of the adoption he had prepared from the very beginning of time. Through the Son this reality of the Father's intention was manifested in action, and the Spirit sent by the Son will bring it to completion in us. Hence, the work of grace is triune. By raising us again together with the Son, the Father has drawn us into the event of divine life happening between the Father and the Son in the Holy Spirit.

The entire work of salvation is and remains to the very end triune grace. Even if this work of God is going to call forth work on our part as well, these works that God shows us how to perform do not acquire any autonomous meaning and motif of their own within the work of grace. Outside of grace they could be neither seen nor done, and even inside of grace they cannot be performed in any sort of independence from grace. They are effects of grace in us, they belong to God, who inspires us to do them and makes them possible in us; they are never our justification before God but always a fruit of this justification. They are meant to be a witness to the truth of the statement: *You have been saved by grace*.

Through faith. Faith is the first effect of grace that comes to light in us, the first work of grace. That we recognize Christ as the Son of God and the redeemer of the world according to the design of the Father is a knowledge by faith. It distinguishes itself from every purely conceptual and intellectual sort of knowledge by the fact that it is a work of grace, an effect in us of the Spirit of God. Without the knowledge of faith, Christ would be nothing for us but a projection of our thought; he would possess the kind of objectivity that the knower designs and posits in one way or another, as a content and a fact that can be true without his having to enter into personal relationship, much less a relationship that requisitions his entire existence. Through faith, Christ is known as the one who came from the concrete God in order to redeem man in the concrete, in order to enter into a most intimate union with me, a union that enables the same miracle of the Father to happen in me as in him: resurrection from the dead and translation into heaven. Grace can have nothing to do with a realm of abstract laws and truths; it is the most real reality, and through faith it grants access to this reality. Faith is that effect of grace that allows us to have a sense of grace and thereby to catch sight of God. It is our part in our salvation, but this part is, of course, grace; it has its origin in God and goes back to God. Through grace, God has entered into an invisible communication with us, but the effect of grace in us is faith, which enables us to enter into it visibly with him. Faith is, so to say, the reflux back to God of what flows out first to us as grace. Thus Paul sees in faith above all grace, even if this grace cannot dispense with our "cooperation". If it were primarily our work, we could produce it of ourselves, we could build the bridges to God ourselves, and, finally, we could redeem ourselves. But in this way we would arrive only at a God excogitated and invented by us. This faith could not flow back to the true God precisely because it would not have flowed out from him. Nor does Paul now speak of cooperation with grace; this was already alluded to where he spoke of our being quickened together in Christ, which presupposed being taken and, consequently, a letting oneself be taken, into life.

Nor is this of you; it is God's gift. No one has the possibility of going to God unless God gives it to him. And this act of giving and bestowing by God has its complete development and full activation when it reaches the beneficiary of the gift and takes effect and unfolds in him. The creature is like the spark that ignites the powder that God gives. Without this gift of God, there would never be any ignition. Man could perhaps form some idea of God and of his gifts, but this would be thoroughly theoretical and lifeless. In order to know God's gifts in truth, one must possess them, that is, possess grace and faith. Grace is like a food that is placed in the creature's mouth and gives the tongue the possibility—this is faith—to taste it as food. God always begins to work by inserting something of himself where he intends to operate. He produced the creature from the outset in such a way that it always remains accessible like this and so that this operation is always assured him. Even when our faith looks like our own deed, which aspires toward God, in reality it is so only because it originates from God and reveals itself in us as God's gift. And when it begins to work in us, it does so just as God predetermined and incorporated it into the gift. If we had to shift for ourselves, we would never be redeemed, that is, would never find the correct approach to God. By giving us faith, God creates this access between himself and us. And in this way it is also clear that no one who does not possess and who has not tasted faith can know what faith is. It cannot be produced, thought out, constructed from man's side; just as one cannot know how a fruit tastes without ever having tried it. And in the last analysis, nonbelievers never have but individual truths and verities, so that even the truth of God and of the Church will always appear to the nonbeliever as a heap of individual dogmas and rites and customs. In the gift of faith, however, God brings about in man the subjective unity of truth, just as he has effected the objective unity of all divine truth in the Son. For faith is participation in the truth and life of the Son. The believer's "eyes are opened", so that he sees the unity of the truth and, by the grace God gives him, experiences it in himself. He thus becomes one with himself, because he has become a partaker of the unity of God in the Son.

2:9. *Not of works, so that no one may boast.*

If we were capable of saving ourselves by our works, this would mean that we were in possession of a power that, applied rightly, would be sufficient to put us in contact with God and to reconcile us to him. The way to God

would then be no longer the Son but our own ego. If
we were our own way, we could be self-sufficient. God
would be the one to whom we aspired out of some feeling
or need, but we would have produced this feeling, this
need, ourselves, fancied its necessity ourselves, chosen
the way ourselves, and, in fine, even God would be our
own work. Thus everything would redound to our glory.
But it is precisely this glory that must under no circumstances be the outcome. Paul says expressly: *not of works,
so that no one may boast.* By boasting, we would in some
way or other have to compare ourselves with God, set
ourselves in opposition to God, survey and evaluate our
relationship to God ourselves, esteem ourselves, therefore, as in some sort standing next to God by equality of
origin, as having importance next to God, as being able
to lay claim to a significance, to a value next to God.
We would divide the honor between God and ourselves;
perhaps in such a way that the lion's share fell to God,
but a modest share alongside his would still be assured
us. Whoever considers God in this fashion has understood nothing about God. He can do it only in unbelief. The glory of the creature, its value, and its claim to
consideration can have their origin only in the fact that
God regards it as praiseworthy, valuable, and deserving of
consideration. And that he does so is his grace. For this
reason the creature's answer can consist in nothing else
but praising God's grace in everything, that is, believing
and making itself a vessel into which God can pour out
his contents. But every way that attempts to go to God
on its own power would inevitably be a path that leads
away from God back to itself. For whoever praises him-

self does not praise God enough and distances himself
from God. Hence, if God redeems us, then he refuses us
the status of instruments of our own redemption.

2:10. *For we are his handiwork, created in Christ Jesus for good
works that God prepared beforehand for us to walk in.*

We are God's handiwork, and we can perform our good
works only by being his work. Everything we work, we
work within our property of being works. Consequently,
work is to a large extent parallel to faith: we can believe
only because God has put faith into us. *Created in Christ
Jesus.* Paul gives to this second creation complete preponderance over the first. We are no longer creatures of the
first creation but creatures of the redemption. Just as God
sent his Son as the second Adam, so too he recognizes
in us now the children of the second covenant. He now
enlarges and extends to us as well his act of generating
the Son and his act of sending the Son to become man;
he wants to behold us as creatures who exist within his
generated Son. Hence, the question here is not the foundation of the first creation in Christ but the new creation through the Incarnation, death, and Resurrection
of Christ.

For good works. Coming from him, we are his handiwork, so that, returning to him, we may do good works.
These works are supposed to help us remain on the path
that leads to God. God *prepared them beforehand*, like mile-
stones, by which we could ascertain the right way. Before
he created us anew in the Son, he had carefully chosen
and made ready the way that was to lead us to God, fixing

the individual stretches of road and marking them with different good works that he expects from us. And just as the way of the Son was a way of obedience, so too our way to him in the Son should be a fruit of the Son's grace of obedience. The works along this way could not be established otherwise than as works of obedience.

That we might walk in them. Paul has now arrived where he was at the beginning of the chapter, only the directions are opposite. Previously we walked away from God surrounded by our transgressions and sins. Now we walk once again toward him in the midst of our good works. If God takes such pains to prepare these works for us beforehand, this is a proof of how indispensably necessary they are and proof that we cannot demonstrate to him the obedience of our faith except by doing in faith and obedience precisely what he expects of us. For these good works are indeed works of faith, but they have received their concrete form from God. God has personally assigned them to each man by *preparing beforehand* the course of each life. Faith is one for all, whereas good works, despite their necessity, possess no such unitary value. Just as sins and transgressions were various and different in each case, so too are the good works that must take their place and that here in Paul look almost like a reverse image of perverse works.

2:11. *Therefore be mindful: you, who were once Gentiles in the flesh, called the uncircumcision by that which is called the circumcision, which is made in the flesh by human hand.*

The community formerly consisted of Gentiles, and what separates them from the Jews is unperformed circumcision. For the Jew of the Old Covenant, circumcision was the sign of belonging to the chosen people. By this rite, which was included in their faith but only one aspect of it, which set a visible seal on men in the same way that the seal of the Holy Spirit imprints upon Christians an invisible character, they justified dividing humanity into two halves. As if for them it were not faith that distinguished them from the Gentiles, but as if the sign in their flesh were the most important thing. Yet it was merely a sign made by human hands. It was supposed to be a sign of their interior belonging to God through faith. By turning the sign into the reality signified, they demonstrated that they lived more according to the letter than to the spirit. By assigning to an insignificant matter the significance that at bottom is due to God alone, they showed that the essence of faith was eluding them more and more.

In the Jews' mind, the Gentiles were the disadvantaged. Yet they did not become accomplices of the Jews' unrighteousness, because they were the condemned and not the judges. For this reason they also have no part in the narrowness of the Jews. They, who do not know God, approach him with a more naïve expectancy than the Jews, who were guilty of a grave confusion.

2:12. That at that time you were without Christ, excluded from citizenship in Israel and strangers to the covenants of the promise, without hope and without God in the world.

The small advantage of the Gentiles was outweighed by a much greater disadvantage. Paul unsparingly depicts for them their condition at the time in order to make the greatness of the grace they have newly received appear to them more clearly. He begins with the worst part of all: they were *without Christ.* The course of their present life as believers is entirely shaped by Christ, and every day their life receives its meaning afresh from him. Paul has just spread out before them the full abundance of the riches of their faith. Looking back from this point, they must call to mind the complete hopelessness of their state at the time, the emptiness of their existence, which today is scarcely imaginable any longer. They have to relive in memory the whole abyss of lostness so that afterward, when the Apostle sketches for them the new Christian way, they may thankfully accept its hardships as a trifling matter. Because they were outside of Christ, their soul was empty. But even their community life was empty, because they were *excluded from citizenship in Israel,* both from its earthly commonwealth as the visible people of the promise and from the citizenship in heaven that it had on the basis of this promise. These heavenly advantages were the *covenants of the promise* between God and the people, to which the Gentiles were likewise *strangers.* Everything that brought meaning and comfort to the Jews' life was withheld from them. Their alienation was not merely a pure not-knowing but the consciousness of not being admitted to something the Jews possessed. Whenever the Jews spoke of the promises, of the covenant, and of the citizenship resting upon it, the Gentiles understood enough to know that there was something here that gave the Jews strength and hope and from which they themselves were excluded. Something incomprehensible to them, but which doubtless contained a core of reality. Their alienation consisted in the fact that they remained *outside*, that they could contact this mysterious reality only from the outside, the reality that again and again closed itself to them every time they approached. Hence, they were *without hope*, for hope was stored precisely in the promise. Their own situation was such that not only in society at large but also in the private sphere they incessantly ran up against boundaries, confines, and walls, a situation where in general everything could be surveyed and calculated. Precisely that was the hopeless thing. Even if they did not know the number of their days, they still knew that they were numbered, and they also knew the most that could still be expected from an earthly life. Beyond that, they could only cherish conjectures, could only construct for themselves images, which, however, turned out to be all-too-transparent projections of their wishes and apprehensions. They were prisoners of their temporality; every rest from this life was forbidden them, every prospect obstructed, every flight beyond themselves to a safe haven impossible. All of this is summed up in the insight that they were *without God in the world*. In a world that appeared to be closed on all sides and that offered no way out toward God. They knew something of the extent of this world, which was many times greater than what they could traverse and encompass and which, nevertheless, could be measured by their own measurement. This world was hopelessly finite, however its parts and aspects might be considered and ranged together. Of a world to which the infinite God stands in relation they knew nothing. Since even the God of this world they could comprehend was not truly living, they knew even less of an incomprehensible world and least of all of a living God in this higher world.

Paul does not speak here of pagan gods and notions of divinity. Partly because as a Jew he does not like to have anything to do with such matters; in part, too, because he does not want to concern himself now with possible positive sides of the earlier paganism, since his present intent is to lead his readership away from false modes of living onto the true path to God. Indeed, he is also speaking now, not—as in Athens—to pagans and unbelievers, but to believing Christians, upon whom he would like to impress the immeasurable distance between then and now, so that they will draw the consequences of this new life without compromise. So he delineates the situation in black and white terms; measured by the God whom they now possess in faith, what they worshipped back then was a nondivinity and their life was godless.

2:13. *But in Christ Jesus you who were once far off have now been brought near in the blood of Christ.*

They were far off in every respect: distant from God, from the promises, from one another, nowhere at home. That which characterized their life most deeply was this estrangement and distance. Everyone had to rely on himself; he did not feel comfortable in sin yet saw no way out that would have opened up to him access to his neighbor or to God. And the estrangement of every individual tended naturally to heighten the estrangement of everyone else: every time they tried to come close to one another, they got in their own way, with the result that every attempt ended in greater estrangement, in the knowledge that they were altogether much more estranged from one another than they had thought.

But in Christ Jesus you have now been brought near. Now they have the lost the feeling of distance from one another, they have come close to one another, have been disclosed and presented to one another, because they have begun to form a communion in Christ Jesus. And everything that hitherto bound them to themselves and caused in them the permanent feeling of alienation has been transformed in the Lord into a connecting bond to God, to God's promises and to one another. And this has happened *in the blood of Christ*, since he shed his blood for them and thereby purchased them for himself, in order to give them to one another as well. Hence, they now live sheltered in the Lord and among one another. The very fact that they are in the Lord at all removes their alienation; that they have been purchased by his blood gives them everywhere nearness and presence, because the blood of the Lord lives in them and binds together everything that separates, makes good every sin in them. This blood has not been poured into the void but received in the Church.

2:14a. *For he is our peace, who makes the two one and has torn down the dividing wall, the enmity.*

The peace, the redemption of the Lord is described here as peacemaking, as reconciliation of what had until now been divided. That which is divided is not at peace, because it has no unity to rest in, because the parts are foreign to one another and cannot unite themselves. By themselves they do not have the chance even to strive for unity, much less to produce it by their own power. But they are even less able to be self-sufficient as parts, to transform themselves into a totality by lying. They feel dimly that they are only parts and that the other part has and is something that in reality concerns them; but they perceive this relationship only as a division, only as enmity.

Unity comes from above, from the Lord. He came in order to establish it, for he has it in himself. He shed his blood in order to penetrate and bring to unity those things that had stood in hostile opposition. This unity is not produced by the natural disposition of the parts that are to be united but lies exclusively in him. He is the unity that actively creates unity, because he is God, and God is triune. Father, Son, and Spirit are one, in an eternal unity and reciprocal unification. Everything that distinguishes them seems to exist only to enable their unity, to deepen it, to bring it into relief. This unity of God is the true and original unity that is the archetype of all unities. On account of sin, our sense for God's kind of unity has been clouded; on the one hand, we confuse unity with lack of articulation and chaotic identification; on the other hand, we consider the Persons in God as units subsisting apart. We rend the mystery of the trinitarian unity, in which being one is the supreme and at the same time most differentiated reality. So that one must even say: the more the Persons in God differentiate themselves, the greater is their unity. And now the Father sends the Son into the world in order to show us how great the divine unity is. For he lives on earth in union with the Father in the Holy Spirit; He is always coming from the Father and going to the Father; the Father is in him and he is in the Father. Because the unity of the Persons in God is not merely a passive or static one, but at the same time comprises the highest power of unification, the Son, by revealing God, goes through the world unifying. In the end, in the shedding of his blood, he consummates this act of unifying by taking into himself everything divided in order to bring it back into its unity with the Father. That he is *our peace* means that he produces in every one of us, but also in every community, in every group, unity tending toward him and, through him, a unity with the unity of the triune God.

The *two* are first the Jews and the Gentiles, but then everything that is two, everything that by nature cannot or will not be one. In this sense, man is two without Christ, because at the same time he both wills and does not will to sin. He is the eternal antagonist of himself. But man and woman, or two brothers or neighbors, two groups with their diverse and opposed intentions, are also two. It is, at bottom, the naked numeral two that becomes the numeral one. One could contemplate the entire life and speech and activity of the Lord from this point of view. Take the parables, for example: the lost sheep, the prodigal son; or else the miracles: how he brings back the blind man into the one light, Lazarus into the one life, Mary and Martha who, separate in their missions, are one in the Lord, the marriage of Cana, where the one wine that comes from the Lord and surpasses every other refreshment is tasted. Even where the Lord divides, he does so for the sake of unity, in order to lay hold of the wicked, who are divided in themselves, from the point of unity by judging them and to lead them to this unity. The Lord often divides only in order to be able to unite better afterward. Or else he dissolves false unities in order to compose the parts in the right way. Everything he takes in hand he unifies toward the Father.

Who has torn down the dividing wall. The wall had been erected by men, who always incline toward divisions wherever they have the chance. They had found occasions for discord and schism everywhere, had partitioned themselves into groups that, in their turn, had managed to erect new, smaller dividing walls within themselves, without ever forgetting that the principal walls, which divided the larger groups, were thereby raised even higher. The whole of humanity had splintered in enmity. The Lord, however, who in every relation to the Father, the Spirit, and men desires peace and wills to draw everything into peace, had to begin by tearing down the walls that are an obstacle to peace. The wall is an obstacle to our understanding of the Lord, who is unity. There is thus a simultaneity of his act of demolition and our act of comprehending. It is as if our most interior walls of division tumbled when he tears down the outer ones. For there is a hidden system, invented by man, that connects the various walls of division to one another and makes them into a great wall erected against God. When the Lord attacks this wall at some point, the whole of it collapses.

The enmity is composed by means of the act of tearing down. The Lord comes with God's friendship, which in turn unites him, as does peace, with the Father, the Spirit, and with men. This friendship, because it is divine, is infinitely greater than human enmity. Even though he gave this friendship human expression on earth, what he offers is still infinitely more than a man's friendship. It is in human guise the offer of friendship on the part of God, who makes the friendship that men return him in their human way enter into his divine and infinite friendship.

2:14b–15. *By annihilating in his own flesh the law of commandments in decrees, in order to create out of the two a new man in himself, bestowing peace.*

The flesh of the Lord is the flesh of a man who at the same time is God. So it is flesh and more than flesh: expression of the divine spirit. His divine spirit, which assumed human form, infuses the Spirit into his flesh. It is not separable from his spirit even in thought, because the Spirit of the triune God perennially vivifies it. When he returns to the Father, he does not leave behind on earth a dead flesh but rather takes his living, spiritual flesh together with his spirit back into heaven, in order to make it from heaven a permanent tool of salvation. He lived on earth the perfect unity of spirit and flesh in order afterward to transmit this unity to us in a living way in the Eucharist.

Whatever he did for us: whether he was being born, in order to take upon himself the burden of our guilt, or whether he was dying on the Cross under this burden, he did it as much with his flesh as with his spirit. In this *flesh he annihilated the law of commandments in decrees*, and did so utterly, because what he had to bring ran counter to this form of the law. The law he encountered had lost its vigor on account of the enormous number of the commandments and decrees. It had become a reflection of and a motive for human enmity. In order to remove from the law this divisive element of enmity, in order to restore to it divine vigor, he had to abrogate it completely by entering into it with his flesh. He formed as it were a unity with this law in his flesh, in order to let both die on the Cross and in his Resurrection to let the law rise anew together with his flesh. Just as before (2:6) he died with man in order to rise and ascend into heaven with him, so now he does so together with the old law, in order to raise it up as a spiritual law. For just as men had once been created by God but by sin fell away from him, so too the law had once been issued by God and then by men's sin had been turned away from its divine origin and its unifying purpose and had been perverted into its opposite. The Lord restores both again. But because the law in its perverted form had become a fleshly human one, the Lord had to institute his fleshly divine law in order to lead us back into the divine spirit.

In order to create out of the two one new man. The Father created man before his countenance. It was the first creation. The second creation is realized in the Son himself. The Son does not multiply the number of creatures, he does not create a second natural life; he creates the old one anew. The Father made creatures come forth from nothing; the Son does not have to annihilate them in himself in order to recreate them in himself out of nothing. He destroys in himself the old Adam, the wall of separation and sin, yet he destroys only after having taken up into himself the thing to be destroyed. He destroys it by dying himself and by letting what he has assumed die together with him. He includes the act of destruction to enable resurrection with him out of the nothing of death. When the Father saw that the old creation was no longer good for anything, he did not destroy it. He was just on the point of doing so in the flood. But, looking ahead to the Son, he let the kernel of the old creation continue in existence in order one day to create it anew together with the Son. The Son has recreated the world, in himself, in his love made flesh, which he offers in order to give to the destruction of sin and division the meaning of love.

The great division in humanity at the time of the Lord's appearance was the division between Jews and Gentiles, and the cause of the division was the fact that the Jews possessed the law, whereas the Gentiles did not. The Lord abolished the boundaries by annihilating the Jewish law in his flesh, so that what could divide them no longer existed. The divided parties were, so to say, once more disposed for a new connection. They had to seek the connection where there had previously been division; since the Lord had taken the cause of division into his flesh, where he had annihilated it, he himself had become the place of the new connection. In this way he *made of the two one new man*, the man who believes in him. This man can live only in him and from him, because he did not create man once for all but also generates him perennially anew, constantly gives him his own substance, without which he could not live. Since the substance of the annihilation of the law was his flesh, the substance of the vivification of the new man is likewise located in this flesh. It is in his flesh, so long as he sojourns as man among men and, in a unity belonging to God's mission, proffers to the newborn men his flesh and his words as nourishment. Even after his return to the Father, it is in his flesh, since he presents the Church with his Eucharist, which bestows life upon us in his flesh and his spirit. For just as the old man drew a substance out of his sin, a substance that enabled him to lead a life against God, so too the new man needed a substance for his new life with God, and this he draws from him who took man's sins upon himself and destroyed them there.

Through this new creation, the Son was *bestowing* peace: between the Jews and the Gentiles, between the man of the Old and the man of the New Covenant, between all erstwhile sinners, who now live in faith. He has bestowed it everywhere by taking upon himself everything lacking peace in order to feed men with his peace, which is the peace of the triune God. This peace is necessary so that the unifying power of the God who puts himself into our hands can be given us in God without disruption and on a permanent basis. He gives us out of the peace of the triune God the peace that he demands of us. The same is true of peace as of love: the Lord gives it to us so that we can give it through him to the Father, the Son, and the Spirit.

2:16. *And reconcile both for God in one body on the Cross,*
killing the hostility in himself.

He cannot reconcile the two in themselves. For in themselves they are divided and incapable of reconciliation.
He must do it in himself, he who is reconciliation in person. He must accomplish the work of reconciliation in
himself so that, proceeding from him, it may take effect
in the two. But in himself means: in his body. For his
body is the expression of the fact that he has come to
us in his spirit of reconciliation, that he has become man
for the sake of reconciliation. Hence, he reconciles the
two into the one body that he is, and in this reconciliation, his body becomes their body. Thus, it is not as if he
reconciled them in himself in order then to release them
again from himself, but since he has reconciled them in
himself, he leaves them the place and the spirit of his reconciliation, which are none other than his body. They
remain in his one body in order to remain reconciled to
one another. Their reconciliation among themselves and
their remaining in his one body are from now on inseparable. If he were to dismiss them again from his body
after the reconciliation, they would immediately fall back
into the old enmity.

By thus reconciling them in his body, he reconciles
them *for God*, with God, and in God. He reconciles them,
not for themselves personally and separately, but for them
already understood in a unity with the Father. For them
as exponents of those whom he has come to reconcile,
for those who not only are fitted out with the dividing
label Jew and Gentile but for him already fall under the

unifying category of sinner. He reconciles them for God the Father so that the Father's joy in his creation may be restored. And also for them, so that they can partake of the joys promised by the Father. He reconciles them, then, so that joy may reign, and joy can reign only if suffering is taken away. Thus, he takes upon himself all of the pain they devise for one another, which they inflict upon one another, which was reserved for them; he does this on the Cross, and suffering the Cross he brings them back reconciled to the Father. By causing the Resurrection of his body, which belongs to them—the body he gives them as a gift just as much in his Resurrection as in his death—he takes them in his Ascension back into the unity of the Father.

Killing in himself the hostility. Hostility needs distance in order to exist. And by setting down his body where the enemies are, the Lord takes the estrangement into himself and creates proximity. Through his proximity he unifies, and by uniting he brings friendship. The former enemies, who have converted to him, can no longer be hostilely disposed to one another, because they meet only in him. Real encounter between believing men is from now on possible only in him. Relations between man and man, group and group, can be of value for believers only within faith. Whatever attempted to go around him, tried to acquire subsistence next to him, could not live. Everything that concerns believers concerns the Lord, passes through him, and meets in him.

2:17. *And he came to announce the glad tidings of peace to you who were far off and peace to those who were near.*

However extensive and ramified the Lord's teaching may be, however numerous the words of his preaching, they can still be summarized in the one message of peace. He came to show humanity the peace in which he lives together with the Father and the Spirit and to bring this peace by order of the Father. A peace such as they did not dare to hope for, a peace that embraces everything because embraced by the triune God, because all of its properties are a direct testimony of its origin. And he brings it to those who, like the community, were *far off* and to those who are *near*, like the Jews, because the concepts of far and near merge without remainder in the unity of this peace. His peace is so strong that it overcomes distance and, in the identical suffering of the Cross, overcomes the smallest as well as the greatest distance. No one can say that the Lord had to suffer less for his sake than for others'; that, since he was already near, the Lord had less trouble with him. In God there is a sort of equalization of distances: God, who wishes only proximity, does not measure the distances. That which does not belong to him is against him. Even if it is true that the Gentiles, compared with the Jews, were far off, because they did not possess the law, measured in terms of the peace the Lord has brought, both were far off, because both were brought close to the Father only through the Cross of the Lord.

2:18. *For through him we both have access to the Father in the one Spirit.*

Since the Incarnation of the Son, there is only one access to the Father, and that passes through the Son. This access was already contained in the promise of the Old Covenant. He who believed in this access drew closer to God. Since it was revealed manifestly through the Son, all that was left to do was enter into the Son. The Son is the *access to the Father*. In him alone and *through him* must we come to the Father, and that includes *both*, these as well as the others. Because the Son came in order to unite, he cannot split into two in God, he cannot open diverse paths to the Father; he is the unity of the access in person, and the Father knows us only when he sees us coming to himself in this unity. For the Father looks continually upon the Son. This goes for *both*: the Jews and the Gentiles, the little sinners and the great, the haters and the lukewarm. Since the Son appeared and became the access, there is in him a kind of preliminary bridging over of all alienating distances—preliminary, because bridged over in advance in the Son, so that he might then bring us back definitively to the Father on the solid ground of this bridge that has been erected. Even though one already lives in the Son, in this world one is still always underway to the Father, in whom the final definitiveness of the access, the state of having arrived, is realized.

We receive access to the Father through the Son *in* the Holy Spirit, who at the same time is the *one* spirit of reconciliation whom the Son brings. Our return is accomplished in the unifying spirit of the triune God, which is the Holy Spirit. He helps us find access to the Son, and he leads us together with the Son to the Father.

2:19. *Thus you are no longer strangers and sojourners but fellow citizens of the saints and members of God's household.*

They were strangers in a much deeper sense than they themselves had guessed. Even if they had felt the strangeness and the lack of a homeland, they still would not have known what it means to be at home and where the homeland is. Only now that they have received the grace of being at home in the land can they judge to what degree they were aliens. It is as if the comfort of being at home were even greater than the past uneasiness abroad. They have been introduced into the new reality not only as *sojourners* but as enfranchised citizens who have their homeland there. The homeland they have found, however, surpasses by far anything they could fancy under this heading; it is a homeland founded in the Son and established in the Son. There they have become *fellow citizens of the saints.* The land into which they come is peopled by saints among whom they are reckoned. If the Son brings men to the Father and thus introduces them into the kingdom of heaven, he must also communicate to them the qualities that are vital in heaven. He must introduce them into the heavenly communion and consequently make them into saints. Fellow citizenship is not only a right or a duty but, before all, a being. God gives sanctity to those who become partakers of his kingdom. He does so because he recognizes the qualities of the Son's holiness in them when the Son brings them to him. They are *members of God's household*, people who belong to God's house, and this is so not only because they need to belong to God's household in order to feel at home, in order to attain the certainty that they have a title to the grace won for them by the Son of being allowed to stay there, but also because God's household needs them. When they became members of God's household, a twofold necessity was fulfilled in them: one that lay in them and one that lay in God, who sent his Son to fetch the world and every single creature back to himself.

2:20. *Built upon the foundation of the apostles and prophets, Christ Jesus himself being the cornerstone.*

When God makes his believers members of his household, he does not introduce them into an empty house but into a well-furnished house that is familiar to men. He had the Son become man so that men might be attracted by his humanity, know him as one of their own; in this way the heavenly home, of which he spoke to them, would take on a hue and form familiar to them thanks to his person in their world. The Son carries this farther, making the prophets, who promised him, and the apostles, who proclaim his teaching, the foundation of his house. When Paul discloses to the community that it is *built upon the foundation of the apostles and prophets*, he does so in order to give them the feeling of familiarity. The framework of this building is already known to them; upon entering they will easily find their way about, for the supports of the new communion are the very ones they have already known for a long time. This is an allusion to the mediating position of the saints in the edifice of the Church. *Jesus Christ himself being the cornerstone*; that could frighten them again, be too big for them. But if the apostles and prophets, men like themselves, are the foundation walls, they have no need to fear. Through those men they will find access to the God-man, who for his part will lead them to God the Father. They know already from the first words of Paul that they have to insert themselves into this; they have their place inside the predestination of the Father, and it is now described to them in greater detail as a place within the edifice. They are to do their part to help in the realization of the Father's intentions for this house. But in helping, they should feel safe and secure, because Paul's word assures them that the house is their own paternal home.

The *cornerstone* supports the foundation, is the sign of beginning and of progress at the same time. In this designation the Lord makes known that his connection to the apostles and prophets is indissoluble. Together with them he forms the solid foundation of the house, and his bond to the prophets is just as strong as to the apostles. That he lets himself be utilized as the cornerstone in the house of the Father reveals his decision even in heaven not only to be one with the Father but to live with those whom he has redeemed in the same unity founded in the Spirit. He makes himself for all eternity the support of the apostles and prophets and all believers built upon them, since he has deigned once and for all to be the cornerstone.

2:21. *In him every building, well constructed, grows into a holy temple in the Lord.*

Just as in the first creation the command was issued to grow upon earth, in the second creation in Christ, everything grows in heaven. As long as the earth stands, heaven must grow, that is, every new creature of the Father is destined to be received into the holy temple of the Son. The Son arranges a place for everyone in his house: all the saints who are in the edifice or enter into it have to fit themselves into the Son's order. The Son does not build without a plan, but everything is *well constructed* according to the decisions of the Father. Stone by stone set according to God's design. This setting and growing, however, take place wholly in the Son. It is he who realizes the Father's intentions in heaven, just as he realized them on earth. By associating men to this, he goes on creating a connection from earth to heaven, he constantly opens access to the Father for believers. He is both in one: access as building, building as access. Introduction and the fostering of growth are one in him. What rises in this way is the *holy temple of God*. It is holy because it corresponds to God's holy intention, because it receives his saints, and because it grows in holiness before the Father's countenance. But it is all these things *in the Lord*. Not only because he is the cornerstone, because he dominates the order in which everything is fitted together, but because the whole existence of the temple, its being and becoming, is established by the life of the Lord. Its visible growth is the visible sign in heaven of the Incarnation of the Son, the lasting monument of the redemption of the world erected in heaven, where it partakes of eternal life. The temple, of which Paul is now speaking, is not the visibility of the earthly Church—he is going to treat of that later—but first of all a kind of recapitulation of the whole effect of the redemption, a first vertical projection into which he will later pencil in the outlines of the visible Church.

2:22. *In which you are also built up as a dwelling of God in the Spirit.*

Every building comes to be in the Lord. And from now on without exception, whether it is a question of earthly systems, of laws, or of heavenly things. The Lord is the center of everything that is found in heaven and on earth, and he keeps gathered in himself all the things the Father has determined to recapitulate in him. Christians, however, from the moment they attain to faith, must let themselves be built up in the Lord; they have to be building material he can work according to his needs. And since their place in the edifice is provided for, the construction cannot be brought to completion without them, and they must therefore let the Lord grow and build in them all the more. The great order Paul has indicated as existing in the heavenly temple is now formed in the individual Christian and in the individual community according to its pattern. In the Christian, since he receives a share in the life of the triune God, though this share can be realized only if he dovetails with the overall plan of the temple and allows himself to be fitted into it. Here, in the temple of the Lord, he receives from the Lord by grace the capacity to take part, a capacity he would never possess by himself. In the community, because it too must accomplish the same construction in the Lord as the individual must accomplish for himself. And no one could be built up individually if he were not simultaneously a member in the context of the community, just as the community could not contribute to the construction if its individual members did not allow themselves to be built up.

As a dwelling of God. God the Father needs a dwelling, and he has it in the Son. Each of the Persons of God dwells in every other and dwells safely at home in him. But if the Father is borne in the Son and the Son has entered into a unity with men, then the Father must also find his resting place in the dwelling of the Son—that very heavenly temple that Paul has described. But the community is to be God's dwelling place *in the Spirit.* In the Holy Spirit, God the Father lives in the habitation of believers. It is the Spirit who fits together the dwelling. Of course, the Father conceived the plan, and the Son carried it out, but it is the Spirit who as Spirit of the Father and of the Son at the same time holds the construction together. He is always a Spirit of remaining, of enduring, of the bestowing of duration. If believers grow up as a holy temple in the Son, the temple receives durability through the Spirit. God, who possesses the spirit of permanence and continuity in the perennial newness of love, effects by his Spirit the continuity of his Spirit in Christians as well. It is also he who preserves the consummated earthly work of the Son. When one of the apostles called by the Lord followed him, this was the work of the Son and of the Spirit. When the apostle remains in the Lord after his departure, this is above all the work of the Spirit: he makes everything about the Lord that occurs only once abide. As man, the Son is to be met in the world, in time and space, in what is always a unique event; he teaches us the sense of these unique, vertical encounters, so that we may learn to understand the permanent, horizontal encounters of the Spirit. In relation to the Son, the Spirit possesses the characteristic of introduction, of recalling the Son, of revelation, just as someone can recall a symphony when the principal motif of every movement is played for him. The Spirit, too, appears vertically: where he appears in relation to the Son: in the baptism of the Son at the Jordan or sent by the Son on Pentecost or descending upon the prophets so they can promise the Son, and so on. But he mediates the diverse verticals of the Son in permanence: he gives what plummets down vertically the dilation of eternity. He gives it already in time simply by inspiring and approving purposes, programs, and life plans when they enable and promise duration in God and are not simply condemned to collapse in on themselves after an initial flush of enthusiasm.

THE POSITION OF PAUL
IN THE WORK OF SALVATION

3:1. *For the sake of which I, Paul, Christ's prisoner for you, the Gentiles . . .*

In this incomplete sentence, Paul lets us know three things: that he is the prisoner of Christ, that he is a prisoner for the Gentiles, and that this is so because the dwelling of God consists of all believers. Whoever surrenders himself entirely to the Lord lives together with him as if chained to him; he attempts to bind his entire freedom into the will of the Lord, just as the Lord did nothing but the will of the Father. To be able to do that, man must live in an immediate proximity to the Lord, must never, as it were, lose him from sight so as never to let slip what the Lord is doing or intending to do precisely at this moment. To live in the will of the Lord requires a surrender of every single minute. It therefore goes without saying that Paul considers himself by reason of his mission to be a prisoner of Christ. One may wonder whether the Lord, who consents to be under the surveillance of believers, is not for his part just as bound to the believer as Paul is to the Lord. Naturally, the Lord is free to do as he will. But he renounces this freedom in order to remain permanently in the circle of his own, in order to be from the time of his Incarnation an example for them and to accomplish his works together with them. Paul takes the incarnate Lord at his word. He fetters himself to him, does not let him go, so that finally the Lord also appears to be fettered to Paul. And if Paul now bears also the exterior, bodily chains of imprisonment, so this imprisonment for the Lord is only a visible sign and symbol of that invisible imprisonment in which he lives together with the Lord and which consists simply in sharing the life of the Son in the Father, being together with him in the Spirit, without ever leaving him, so that in the end, when Paul sits in an outward prison, the Lord shares even this with him.

For you, the Gentiles. The community must know that the Apostle lies in chains on their account, that he includes the Gentiles in his mission, that he lives for the conversion of the Gentiles in the Lord. No one can let himself be converted in order just to love the Lord personally; he must undertake the commission the Lord wills to give him. The Lord accepts no offer from a believer in which the commandment of love of neighbor is not fulfilled in some form or another. Even the most purely contemplative mission of adoration will be right only when it possesses an opening toward communion: interiorly, in that the others are included in prayer; exteriorly, in that they know about this mission and are edified by it. In Christian terms, pure solitude with God would be at best a novitiate, an initiation into a later active or contemplative vocation in the Church. Paul sets great store by the fact that the Gentiles know he is in chains for their sake. In this knowledge there is a participation in Paul's sacrifice.

For the sake of which. That is, so that God's dwelling may be possible in them. Hence, the Apostle takes upon himself sacrifice and suffering in order to lighten the way for believers and so that the intention of the Lord might be realized: to construct the dwelling place of God out of all those who believe. Everyone who knows about the house must immediately let himself be fitted into it, must place himself as a living stone at the disposition of the cornerstone; otherwise, whenever he pointed to the house of God, he would always only be indicating the holes he does not fill.

3:2. *If indeed you have heard of the dispensation of the grace of God that I received for your sakes.*

Paul hopes that the community has heard what he is doing for them and what God has given him for them. It would be a relief for him in his incarceration to know that his work is bearing fruit in them. He would obviously take being a prisoner much harder if he had to do without the consolation of this knowledge. God has dispensed graces that were destined for the Gentiles, which the Apostle has received as a mediating vessel, and together with these graces he received knowledge about them. He received this in a personal manner intended for him by God, which he, after having gathered and understood it, must pass on in the manner that seems appropriate to him. In the tasks the Lord communicates to his own, he expects them to transmit these tasks according to their power of comprehension, their reason, and individual character.

Paul was assigned a *dispensation of grace*, hence, a bestowal of grace in a definite arrangement, configuration, and administration, in a definite form adapted to Paul and particularly to his mission and to the recipients of the graces mediated by him. Thus, when a sacrament, confession, for example, is dispensed, the full objective grace can be distributed to every penitent, but in each case, without prejudice to its objectivity, in a form corresponding to his subjectivity, indeed, in the always unique character of the turning of God's subjectivity toward this unique man. This is so here too as well: the economy of grace of which Paul speaks means that the subjectivity with which he apprehends grace and the particular manner in which grace gives itself to him are the vessel and the form of the objective message of grace that he—in his apostolate, which is at once objective and subjective —is commissioned to convey. But there is also a reobjectivization after the passage through the subject, otherwise there would be a great danger that man would measure grace according to the subjectivity of reception, according to the feelings and experiences he has in receiving. The Christian has to find the track that leads out of these secondary, subjective reactions back into the objectivity of grace. In the same way Paul, too, must finally convey the grace he apprehends with its highly pronounced Pauline character in such a way that, despite passing through his personality, it remains the objective grace of *God*. Even if he knew that his addressees had much less distinct and acute powers of perception than he, that compared with him they were color-blind, he would nevertheless have to convey in an objective mode of translation what he has experienced. The subjectivity of the apostle is only an instrument of his objective mission, and the subjectivity of his mission is once again only an instrument of the dispensation of the objective grace of God. Missions have a quasi-sacramental character; for the mission is also the objective speech of God in the Church, a word placed in the hand of heralds. Whoever has received a differentiated mission—and he has, after all, received it for the sake of the generality—must be especially careful, despite the personal coloring he is to have, not to take on the airs of a primadonna in the distinguished position he must occupy; he must rather always behave as objectively and catholically-universally as possible. The essential corrective for those sent is a good confessor and counsellor. And wherever the apostle is forced to expose himself personally, he must as soon as possible withdraw again into objectivity. The apostle is like a numeral that is borrowed in addition ("write six and carry one") and that, as soon as it is no longer needed, has to disappear again. Just as in confession the subjective depictions and avowals of sin are rendered objective by the confessor and the sacrament of confession, in the same way all graces corresponding to a personal mission must first be depersonalized by obedience to the spiritual director. One who has a mission should not venture into the community to serve it according to personal judgment but only under the guidance of one appointed to that office and in obedience. Only then is the danger that his own ego might move into the foreground truly banished.

3:3. *By means of revelation the mystery about which I have written in brief above was made known to me.*

Paul has thus come to know about this mystery in a manner designed personally for him—by means of revelation. He does not depict this manner; he limits himself to mentioning its existence, while he keeps its particular character to himself. And as far as the content of revelation is concerned, he has already declared it in summary form; he does not describe this revelation so that the community can test it or judge the manner of revelation, or compare it with other revelations. It must be satisfied with knowing that Paul has a relationship to God that God uses to communicate insights to him.

It is obvious from his words and from what he has already told them that Paul does not simply repeat what everybody knows but gives news, which, however, is not in contradiction with these already-known facts. Yet it is important to him that he be known as the source of this news; this is part of his mission. He has received revelation from God, and he passes it on in the way that seems suitable to him, without relating the circumstances under which God spoke to him or depicting possible conditions under which he was given the task of conveying it, the distinction between what was intended for him and his mission alone and what is meant to be announced to all alike.

About which I have written in brief above. He could, then, have written in greater detail. Neither does he betray the reason why he did not do so. He pulls back a part of the veil in order to draw the other that much closer. But the little he does offer is important, and the community must bear it in mind: what it hears from him is not his personal opinion, but revelation. But it is only a hasty synopsis of the whole, which is certainly greater than what it gets to know. And yet the community cannot procure the supplement from another source, precisely because it is revelation.

3:4. *When you read it, you can form an idea of my insight into the mystery of Christ.*

Paul wants the community to form an idea of his insight, because he wishes it at all costs to bestow confidence upon him, to take encouragement from his strength. Men in the Church need support in order to remain steady on their feet; and one of these supports is the revelations God gives to his elect. Paul knows he owes a great part of his zeal, fidelity, and perseverance in suffering to his revelations. The community is at a disadvantage with respect to him on this score; it must obtain indirectly from him what he has received directly, firsthand from God. But in order to have as full as possible a share in this, it must be convinced of the authenticity and moment of these revelations. Paul is therefore very eager for the community not to underestimate his insight. He uses his revelations, in other words, in two ways in regard to his apostolate: first, in order to communicate them to the community and to impart to it the understanding of them, but also to set himself off from the community, to establish an authority in it, and to let it know that he has penetrated far more deeply into the mystery than it has.

Into the mystery of Christ. The mystery of Christ is here designated as the central point of his revelations. Paul has received insight into the growing edifice of the Lord and of his saints in heaven. The evangelists have recounted what the Lord did, said, and suffered on earth and what as believing men they could learn of this in their communion with the Lord. The revelation of Paul is a continuation of theirs, no longer on earth, but from the Ascension of the Lord onward. He is no longer in a position to see and experience and verify the truth of the Lord with his senses, as did the first disciples—as John will also start from hearing, seeing, touching—his revelation is a revelation of the Lord from heaven, in which the earthly mystery of the Lord is once more illuminated from above and in a vast expansion. Hence, Paul takes pains to do two things: to translate heavenly things in such a way that men can understand something of them, but also to convey a feeling of how much the greatness of the heavenly vision exceeds everything earthly. And the community must perceive the authenticity of this revelation precisely through its incomprehensibility. His silence is a part of his declaration and translation. The greatness of revelation lies in part in what he says and in part in what he is: he lets a glimmer of its splendor irradiate back onto himself, in order to secure for himself the authority of the mediator of revelation. This authority was conferred upon him in the revelation, but he must himself look for means of getting it across when the time comes to translate it.

3:5. Which in former generations was not made known to the sons of men as it has been unveiled now in his holy apostles and prophets in the Spirit.

With these words, Paul enrolls himself in the group of those to whom God reveals his mystery. He thereby assures himself once more of the confidence of the community. Even though his insight is great, it does not stand alone; he shares it, on the one hand, with the apostles who lived together with the Lord and received his revelations on earth; he also shares it with the prophets, with those Christians endowed with prophetic gifts who, following the first apostles, receive a sort of continuation of the earthly revelation of the Lord. Paul applies to both the appellation *holy*, naturally in a sense that sets them off from others and that does not coincide exactly with the sense he ascribes to all the faithful. The coming of the Lord and the beginning of the New Covenant signaled a sudden inbreaking of the whole divine truth into the world, a revolution in faith. This prodigious novelty could not be taken in and assimilated all at once, especially since the first apostles, the eyewitnesses of his earthly existence, necessarily remained bound in great measure to his earthly mode of appearance. And this is why it was appropriate that, after the Ascension of the Lord, the time of revelations should continue, that the fragments gathered by the first disciples should be pieced together, supplemented, given a new form, and interpreted, that the one truth of the Lord should be refracted and interpreted in the mirror of manifold revelations. Paul speaks of holy prophets as naturally as he speaks of holy apostles, and he presupposes that the community knows such prophets. He even places himself in their number in order to give himself greater support and to diminish possible mistrust.

The *former generations* lived only in the promise in which such an abundance of revelations was not yet possible. The revelations of that time were more confirmations of the promise, which was forgotten again and again, than absolutely new revelations. Now, however, the entire content of the mystery of Christ can be interpreted down to its various aspects. The *spirit* of revelation, however, is at all times the same: the Spirit of the triune God. The Spirit adapts himself in the divine order to the needs of God. He makes himself available for revelation where the triune decision is already present.

3:6. *That, namely, the Gentiles are coheirs and members of the same body and cosharers of the promise in Christ Jesus through the gospel.*

Paul once again summarizes briefly the quintessence of the revelation that has fallen to his lot: the entitlement of the Gentiles in the New Covenant. In the eyes of the Jews, the pagans were much farther removed from the promise than they, since it was to the Jews that the promise had been issued. It was necessary to have faith in God in order to hear the promise at all. For this reason the Jews also held the opinion that the fulfillment of the promise would concern themselves above all. The mystery of the promise was *their* mystery, and there was no apparent reason why the mystery of the fulfillment should not likewise remain their property. But this facile conclusion proved false. The particular promise becomes universal in its fulfillment: the Son comes for all. The Gentiles stand together with the Jews as *coheirs* of the promise, although they did not possess it when there was nothing but the promise. The whole heavenly inheritance, which the Father gave the Son, is meant just as much for them as for the Jews. Since they have been appointed coheirs, they have no need, either, to take the Jews' former way of approaching the New Covenant from the Old; they acquire an immediate share in the entire fullness. For they are *members of the same body*. In the Incarnation, the Lord assumed the same body they too possess, in order to bring back to the Father in his own body both the body of the Jews and that of the pagans.

Applied to the Church, this would mean: the mediation that leads to God is always chosen by God himself. Mediation through Christ, through the apostle, and through the prophets and saints of the New Covenant is always of such a nature that it is decided and instituted by God himself. No more than their promises and traditions give the Jews the right to place demands on God regarding the future mode of mediating salvation does the Church have this right in the New Covenant. She can—prescinding from the commissioning of men to office, which is the Church's duty—only lay down rules for discerning true mediation from false. She does that insofar as she is *one body* with the Lord.

And copartakers of the promise in Christ Jesus. At the moment it was fulfilled, the promise transcended the stage of the promise, and as such it belongs to the past. Therefore, the Gentiles, who partake of the present fulfillment of the promise, had, as long as it was only promise, a sort of unconscious share in it. Since the promise is in fact fulfilled for them, there was, consequentially, a promise for them of which they were quite unaware. The *gospel* is the source from which they acquire a retroactive share even in the promise, for, as the revealed word of God in the Incarnation of Christ, it is fulfillment. In the Son's becoming man, it is revealed that from all eternity the Word of God was the Son. He remains word but, as such, assumes flesh in order to be word in the flesh and to be seen and understood by us. At the time of the prophets, the word could indeed be heard, but only in the form of a promise; even the word's capacity to be heard had the quality of promise; it was thus promised and promising at the same time. In Christ, on the contrary, it is fulfilled according to content and form, not, indeed, in himself (the Word always was fulfilled), but for us. That is the gospel.

3:7. *Whose servant I have become by the gift of God's grace, which was bestowed upon me through the virtue of his power.*

Paul terms himself a servant of the gospel, that is, not a servant of the Lord only; otherwise, his activity would move only within the insights and revelations given him by the Lord: the Lord as a person would be the central point from which the revelations would irradiate, as it were. But now Paul is a servant of the gospel, in the sense described before. The gospel becomes the central point and therefore also the measure and criterion of what he knows of the Lord and what is revealed to him about

the Lord. It is an objective center, which is at his disposal
and at the disposal of all the faithful, and to which Paul is
related like every other believer. In relation to the gospel,
he does not have a special position, as he does in the case
of the revelations. And this special position is justified
only if it throws him again and again back into the center
of the gospel. He is a *servant*, and his service consists in
understanding and proclaiming what the gospel, the message with which he has been charged, contains. He can
no more take so much as one step away from the gospel
in his service than can anyone else.

He did not become a servant on his own initiative but
by the gift of God's grace. Hence, it is a distinction to be a
servant, specifically, a distinction that lies with grace, for
which the recipient of the gift can only give thanks. Service is a form of receiving a gift. But he who receives it
is obliged *by the virtue* of the *power* of this divine bestowal
of grace. The answer of the one called is the sign of the
efficacy of God, since of himself he would not have the
strength and possibility to accept. Whenever God gives
a gift that comes from grace, he gives simultaneously the
grace to accept this gift. But if the one called has accepted
thanks to the virtue of God, then this virtue remains in
him: even the fruit of this grace is grace; even the fruit
of this virtue is virtue. Just as the priest possesses an objective authority in virtue of his ordination, an authority that is the authority of God in him, so too, by a certain analogy to the priest, everyone who receives a divine
mission has in himself a power and virtue of God, which
derives, not from the power of his answer, but from the
objective operation of God in him.

3:8. *Upon me, the least of all saints, the grace was bestowed to announce to the Gentiles the unsearchable riches of Christ.*

Paul now discloses the whole contrast between the person of one who is sent and his mission. He calls himself here the least of all saints. He knows himself and knows who he is and thus knows that those who believed in the Lord and staked their lives on him were and are all greater than he. He belongs, of course, to the communion of these saints, he who has been sanctified by his faith and his mission, but as the least. In spite of that, *this grace was bestowed upon* him, this unheard-of mission was entrusted to him: to proclaim the Lord to the Gentiles, who until the coming of the Lord knew nothing or wanted to know nothing of God. But not a Lord who had lingered insignificantly in their midst, of whom they might have thought little, but the Son of God, who possesses *unsearchable* riches. The Lord takes the Gentiles seriously; he wants to give himself entirely to them. Paul receives the task of announcing to them this totality. He is to make it clear to them how seriously God takes them, show them everything that can be searched, and among these things is the property that the riches of Christ are unsearchable. In order to be able to do both things, he must throw himself entirely into the service of the Gentiles, into this service of the knowledge of the Lord and of the Lord himself. So that it also becomes evident how much the Lord demands the utmost even from his least saints but also places this utmost at their disposition as a grace, so that they can fulfill their mission.

3:9. And to bring to light what is the dispensation of the mystery that was hidden from all ages in God, who created all things.

From all eternity God has hidden mysteries in himself: even where he revealed himself, there was nonrevelation alongside his revelation, whether one guessed its existence or not. One could only say that there were sure to be hidden mysteries in God, mysteries that were not in contradiction with the ones that were revealed, because there is no contradiction in God. And now it is Paul's office to bring into the light of revelation mysteries that from eternity were hidden in God. This light is given by God himself in order to illuminate his mystery. The God who reveals himself is the God *who created all things* in the same perfect freedom with which he now communicates the mystery, in the same perfect power with which he creatively orders the dispensation of revelation.

What is revealed is the *mystery* that does not cease to be a mystery on account of being dispensed. Only previously it was *hidden*. And now it is revealed. In such a way, in fact, that the Apostle has to comprehend what is shown him and, in his comprehension, has the task of communicating it. Paul is thus inserted in the middle of the event of revelation; receiving, he must transmit, not, however, mechanically, but in such a way that through him it is brought to light. He is forbidden to transmit it obscurely; he is given enough understanding and light to be able to bring forth on his own light and understanding in men. This understanding does not so thoroughly clear up the mystery that it stops being a mystery; its reference point is not least of all this mystery-character: one understands in the clear light of God that it is a mystery. It is, for example, clear that Mary conceived the Son of the Father by the working of the Holy Spirit, but this fact does not cease to be infinitely mysterious. It even becomes all the more sublime, many-sided, and mysterious, the more the believer penetrates into it, the more he understands of it. In God, our clarity, compared to his, is still and all the most obscure concealment, while our hiddenness is the most perfect clarity in him. We know that God is love. But who is God in the first place? And what is the nature of love? And what does "is" mean when it is used of God's being?

3:10. *So that the multiform wisdom of God may now be made known to the principalities and powers in the heavens through the Church.*

Much of the wisdom of God and its multiformity was already revealed in the Old Testament and in the gospel. But the sense of Paul's commission is to disclose this manifold form even further. It is precisely *wisdom* that he has to make known; everything he reveals of God's mystery must be an expression of wisdom. It is variegated and *multiform*; it cannot be taken in with a single glance; it is not limited to a single track, but in all directions is surprising and infinitely inflected, so that the mystery is, as it were, not only a quantitative but also a qualitative mystery. Paul's commission is not of a purely personal sort but, because he is a servant of the gospel, has its place within the Church. Thus, the point is now the synthesis between his commission and that of the *Church*. When he speaks, he does so in virtue of the wisdom communicated by God. One cannot speak of it wisely without being a partaker of it, but God bestows wisdom on the Apostle and upon the Church simultaneously. The Church does not get God's wisdom by circumventing Paul, and Paul does not get it by circumventing the Church. Paul receives it in the Church, and the Church receives it in Paul. Paul has as an apostle the peculiar position in which the revelation he receives is mediated to the Church through him and is authoritatively binding on the whole Church. Yet the mystery is not exhausted by its exposition; God can again and again illuminate and reveal aspects of it later on as well. This, too, will occur in a simultaneity with the Church, although not with the authority of the apostle, so that the Church will be competent to test such revelations, which she may not do in the case of the apostle. Paul possesses this simultaneity with respect to the Church on the basis of his office, of his service to the gospel. In him, office and person are so fused that every bit of God's wisdom that affects him personally also concerns him officially and thus ecclesially.

Through the Church, the *principalities and powers* in the heavens are now to become conversant with the wisdom of God. There is not only the immediate way from God to man and from man to God. There is also the way from God via the heavenly spirits to men. As a way of prayer, the grace of which comes from God but which we direct toward the dwellers of heaven, soliciting their intercession, this way is already familiar to us. But the way of prayer can also be a way of revelation, so that

God communicates wisdom to the inhabitants of heaven through man in the Church; gives to the Church, and consequently to her office, a commission that on occasion is intended, not for men, or not for them alone, but also for the dwellers of heaven. By acting in this manner, God shows that he has not given the Church the character of a transitory institution but that he rather admits her into a connection with and dependence upon heaven both in her receiving and in her giving. If, then, in virtue of the Church, Paul receives a revelation because he exercises office in the Church, and this revelation is intended not only for the earth but also for heaven, so too the Church, which was instituted to connect man to heaven, can bindingly promulgate her wisdom and decrees in heaven as well, and she does it inasmuch as this possibility to bind and to loose in heaven as on earth belongs without qualification to her office.

Paul introduces the Church relatively late in his letter. At the beginning, the whole of revelation seemed to take place between God and the Apostle alone. It is as if Paul saw the Church first in heaven, in the Lord, then to a considerable degree formed and represented by his own person, and only afterward, as a by-product of his apostolate, when in coordination with him she receives revelation. As long as the Lord sojourned on earth, the Church lived in him. When he ascended into heaven, he took her in some sense up with himself, and Paul descries her first in heaven. But when he is sent out in mission and office, Paul suddenly discovers the whole earthly side of the Church; he brings her back to earth, a little like Moses brings back the tablets from the mountain, and he sees her now in her earthly aspect working from earth toward heaven.

3:11. *According to the eternal intention that he has carried out in Christ Jesus, our Lord.*

All of God's intentions have existed since eternity. God cannot be constrained by any temporal situation to alter his intentions. Although they seem in our eyes to be conditioned as if by external circumstances, in reality they are closed up tightly in his eternal decree. Whenever we see him perform a determinate act, we know that it was eternally in his intention to execute it at a given moment.

He has made known his wisdom through the Church, in an eternal decree that *he carried out in Christ Jesus.* The Son came so that the wisdom of the Father might be revealed through the Church. If the Father carries something out through the Son, this means that the Son carries out the will of the Father, and this will of the Father, which now comes to life and is expressed in him, is the same will in which the Father had made his decrees from eternity, knowing that the Son, through his obedience, would enable him to realize them. But this Son is *our Lord* and stands as such in the Church. When the Church makes known something of the wisdom of God, she does it through her Lord, who is her head. Head and body are so closely connected that, when something is realized by the Church, it is realized by the Lord; and when the Lord has to do something in his responsibility for the Church, he does it, not as a detached individual, but as the one before whose feet the Church was laid as his fullness.

3:12. *In whom we have boldness and access in confidence through faith in him.*

What we receive in the Son we have received through faith; the Son, who in himself is unvaryingly the same, modifies the effect of his properties in relation to us when we come to faith. Without faith, we could not comprehend whom we have before us or, for the same reason, what he has to give us. Faith, however, which reveals him to us, reveals to us what he has to give us and at the same time conveys to us his gifts. Through faith we have *boldness and access in confidence*, gifts that are comprised in the Son's eternal return to the Father. All his gifts really take full effect only when they lead back to the Father and are presented to him; they have acquired this property from the Son's return. *Boldness,* unabashed candor, natural openness: the Lord gives us these characteristics of all children along with the grace of sonship. Children do not have to ask first whether they are welcome; they are naïve and unselfconscious, because they always have *access in confidence* to their father. From the moment the Son assumes us, we no longer need to ask for the hour when we may enter the Father's presence. The Father's hour is the hour of the Son. And this struck as soon as we reached the Son by faith. On the basis of the Incarnation, our whole relationship with God has been, as it were, rerouted: our questions and doubts about the Father are now directed to the Son, who resolves them by giving us faith and who gives us the Father in himself, with a naturalness characteristic of the Son. He gives us the unaffected ease and confidence that as eternal Son he has toward the eternal Father to demonstrate that through him and in him we have become real children of God.

3:13. *Therefore I beg you: Do not be discouraged on account of my afflictions for your sake, for they are your boast.*

After Paul has described his mission in relation to the Gentiles and within the Church, he reverts to his imprisonment. He does not wish to depict his afflictions. He merely uses them as an occasion to formulate a request: *Do not be discouraged on account of my afflictions.* They must not let their spirits droop in thinking that the Apostle has been taken away from them and perhaps will no longer be able to help them because his affliction is too great. In reality, the affliction of one sent on mission should never be a cause for believers to lose heart. It appertains to the Cross of the Lord. Paul knows this so well that he adds: *for they are your boast,* that is, the fruit on which the community can count when it is itself afflicted. It has only to call to mind that someone is suffering for it, and it will realize that the suffering of one believer redounds to the glory of many. Its faith and all faith's properties are strengthened by this suffering and are augmented in boldness and confidence. By means of this suffering, Paul furnishes it tangible evidence that he has a mission to fulfill in its regard, a mission that lies not only in his words but also in his Christian act of enduring. If the very words he writes to them are so full of consolation for them, his chains and his affliction give them the certainty that his words are true. In this sentence, the Apostle finds himself quite close to the corroboration of the whole Christian truth in the Cross of the Lord. The Crucified gives Paul a participation in his suffering by allowing him, too, to be afflicted for the sake of those entrusted to him. That is the boast of the community, what it can rely on, what gives it full surety, what finally distinguishes it before God himself. Appearing before God's judgment, it will be able to point out that the apostle Paul suffered for it, that he paid for a part of its guilt. Paul is perhaps the first who comes to know this form of cooperation; but he limits it at first to himself; he is not conscious that he could have imitators in this property.

3:14. *Therefore I bend the knee before the Father.*

Just as the Son goes from the Cross to the Father, so Paul goes from his affliction to the Father, in order to give him the glory in everything. He does not go alone, he goes together with the Son, because the Son takes him along, because no believer can carry his cross otherwise than in the Son. This communion extends to the fruit of the Cross as well. As the Son brings the entire fruit to the Father for him to dispose of, so Paul, together with the Son, gratefully brings his affliction and its fruit to the Father together with the Son. He bends his knee before him, so that before the ever-greater Father he may become ever smaller. He knows that the Cross and the fruit of the Cross are grace; grace for which he has to thank the Father and which has its origin in the grace the Father apportioned to the Son on the warrant of the Incarnation and of the Cross. As the Son let himself be crucified in order to be abased before the Father, Paul kneels before him in the dust. He kneels because he has become the boast of the community and does not wish to keep this glory for himself. He gives it back to the Father. He gives back to the author of grace the grace shown to him: to participate in the community's conversion and in the securing of its faith.

3:15. *From whom all paternity in heaven and on earth takes its name.*

Paul knows, as he suffers for the community, that he has a relationship of fatherhood in its regard. But no man can be a father without himself being descended from a father and having a relationship to a father. As he exercises fatherhood in faith toward his Gentile communities, Paul has the consolation of being able to return to the Father *from whom every paternity in heaven and on earth takes its name*, who himself has given him faith and the affliction of faith. There is fatherhood on earth in the traditional sense, as Adam became a father after God had generated him. And there is fatherhood in heaven, as God the Son has the Father as his eternal Father; and there is Christian fatherhood, which brings heavenly fatherhood to the earth. On earth, the Church is the expression of the heavenly fatherhood of God the Father. For if she appears as the bride of the bridegroom, then with him she has God the Father as her Father; she shares with the Son this property of being able—together with all who in her are of one body—in faith in God, Father, Son, and Spirit, to see in God her Father. But bridegroom and bride do not stand only in a relation of sonship to the eternal Father; for, like everything in Christianity, even the paternal principle is given away as a grace. By bringing the Father to his Church and bringing his Church back to the Father on the Cross, the Lord assumes a fatherly role toward her and represents the Father for her. Because he places his Cross into the midst of the Church, he gives his Church a share in this fatherhood: by suffering together with the Lord, the Church assumes in relation to her children a share in Christ's fatherhood. The Church transmits in turn something of this property to all those who believe and suffer in her, in the manifoldness of all the Christian possibilities she contains by God's gift. Paul, who bends the knee before the Father as a prisoner, does so in the Son for the Church and in the heart of the Church, on behalf of all for whom he is permitted to be father.

3:16. *That he may grant you to grow powerfully in strength according to the riches of his glory through his Spirit in the inner man.*

Paul does not pray in his prison for himself, for enough strength to endure his suffering. He prays for the strengthening of those entrusted to him. He knows how rich God is. And he asks him to give them this strengthening *according to the riches of his glory*, in the superabundant way that only God can. In order to imagine God's glory, we proceed from what is known to us in the world and attempt to imagine it infinitely enhanced. But this never leads to a real idea of *his glory*. Yet, God is asked here to give strengthening according to the inconceivability of *his* ever-greater glory. The community has to *grow powerfully in strength*, and to grow in strength in the Christian sense always means: to grow stronger toward God, to draw from *his* strength, in order to do what he requires. Not to do it with a force that we could draw out of ourselves, but in the force that he bestows. To grow strong in a strength that he both demands and gives at the same time, gives *through his Spirit*. For the Spirit performs God's works, mediates his glory, sets it in movement toward man, a movement of which one can guess that the whole of God's glory is the cause of the transformation in the Church and in the community.

In the inner man. Their growth in strength must make them men who possess the force by which they live in their inner dimension, ultimately in God. The ordinary man might think that if he grew in strength it would be in an outer man, that the signs of his strengthening would be evident to all: works that elevate him in the eyes of others, positions that are tied to great regard. Paul knows as a believer that when man grows in strength this can happen in Christ only in an inner man. That the inner man is the strongest, because he lives from his faith and this faith is communicated to him by the triune God, who gives him with faith a share in his own strength. A divine force, in relation to which every human force seems null and ridiculous.

The community is newly converted; it stands at the beginning of its Christian course. Paul therefore prays for what developing Christians need the most. If they are to carry out the new will of God, they need above all the divine strength. It is the same here as with all other Christian properties: in order to possess them, one must get them from God. But in conferring them, God gives them with a character that is proper to them in his divinity. The strength of the inner man will be that he possesses inwardly the strength of God, according to the riches of God's glory.

3:17. *So that Christ might dwell in your hearts by faith, you who are rooted and firmly grounded in love.*

On earth the Lord had a dwelling and changed his dwelling. It is as if by dint of the human habit of moving into dwellings he had contracted a heavenly habit of continuing to dwell on the earth. But because he lives once more in unity with the Father and the Spirit, in the Spirit he now dwells in men. The place wherein he can dwell is their heart. By this dwelling, the Lord makes it easy for them to persevere in faith. For this reason Paul prays for this dwelling of the Lord in his followers. They must know that the Lord dwells on earth in them even after his return to the Father, that, when they look for him, they find him in themselves, not in a finite, closed way that would be a pretext to be occupied with themselves and with their heart, but in a heavenly fashion that includes what belongs to it on earth. Dwelling in them, he will disclose heaven to them, since he does not abandon heaven by dwelling in them. Because it is his will that his believers be in his *love* and because his love is *firmly grounded* in the Father and in the Spirit, through his dwelling he draws believers into his love. It is as if he set up in their hearts individual dwellings that are all drawn into the one heavenly dwelling of the Father. He draws their hearts to the Father.

He does this once again *by the faith* that lives in them. If they did not believe, he could not be in them. He prepares his dwelling in them by giving them the gift of faith, which, so to say, furnishes their inner man and makes him habitable, in order to receive the Lord. Faith's role here is to prepare the way: if it is present, the Lord can move in and draw us toward the Father.

Rooted in love. Believers have been sunk like roots into love; love is their earth, their fertile soil. Their entire man is nourished by love through such roots. But to be rooted means at the same time to be *firmly grounded*; they are held fast and made firm by love. Love is for them the only wholesome soil, their fixed habitat, their most intimate homeland; and this love is the love of the triune God, the love that created them, the love that gave them new birth and gives them the strength of enduring perseverance. It is the ground and soil of their development and growth. It has become a vital necessity for their inner man, for God himself has engrafted them in the site of his love and allows them to grow and develop there.

3:18. *That you may be enabled to comprehend together with all the saints what is the breadth and the length and the height and the depth.*

No believer can comprehend anything by himself. He can comprehend because the Lord dwells in him, and even then he can do it, not as an individual, but *together with all the saints*. For the Lord, who dwells in him and enables him to comprehend, simultaneously bestows the same capacity on all the saints, since he lives in all of them. But this comprehension is brought about, on the one hand, by the Lord dwelling in the saint and, on the other hand, by the individual believer's participation in the common comprehension of all the saints, by which it becomes an affair of the Church as well. It is the concern of the Lord as well as of the believer and of the communion of all believers. Thanks to this communion in comprehension, the individual is strengthened, directed, and confirmed in his comprehension. This does not mean that he could not and ought not to comprehend personally and in a unique way. But he comprehends within the congeniality of a communion of truth. The truth already exists: in the Lord, in the Church, and in her saints; and everyone who comes to faith enters into this common space of truth, is strengthened and directed, and will himself bestow upon it strengthening in his turn with his own new, personal coloration. But the origin of the truth that is communicated is God, who is the only one who understands the plenitude of truth, who helps individuals and the community in its developing comprehension, and who steers all of this comprehension back into the incomprehensibility of the infinite God.

Paul opens this space of God when he speaks of four dimensions and requires the introduction into all four. To be introduced into only one would not suffice. It is a question of the breadth and length and height, but also of the depth. Dimensions, however, are not closed spaces but directions, which of themselves point ever farther. So that length is surpassed by length and breadth by breadth, every dimension is raised in intensity by itself, yet each one also bestows further infinities upon the others. Paul knows that his new Christians thirst for knowledge, and he opens to them all spaces. They must come to know God in the infinity of his love. But they must not content themselves with a vague, superficial representation but must push forward in haste from space to space and seek to enlarge their knowledge from dimension to dimension. The opening up of the four dimensions points at the same time toward order and toward infinity. Just as they must not content themselves with a vague knowledge, so too they must not think to reach at any point a conclusion. If the Lord's dwelling in them has impressed upon them any sense of love at all, then they will know that every Christian cognition opens new perspectives, necessitates further seeking, that in the breadth, height, length, and depth of God everything is related to everything else. In the world there are three dimensions. By adding depth as a fourth, Paul does not permit the calculation to leave no remainder. Nevertheless we must be enabled to comprehend. Hence, no other prospect can be held out to us than a progressive endeavor into the infinite. This unattainability of a definitive goal is no reason for Christians not to comply with a clearly expressed command.

3:19. *And to know the love of Christ that transcends knowledge, so that you may be filled with all the fullness of God.*

In the Lord's Incarnation, in his sojourning among us,
in his words and deeds, his love for us was expressed in
a way we could grasp. Knowing the forms of this love
that can be grasped, the Christian also realizes that they
are produced by that love which dwells not only in the
world but also in God and which therefore remains not
only comprehensible but also eternally greater and incomprehensible—the love with which God the Father loved
us from eternity in the Son. Whoever speaks of Christ's
love must include mention of the triune love among Father, Son, and Spirit. When Paul opened just now the
whole range of the four dimensions, he was ultimately
talking about God's triune love, which transcends all understanding, as it was revealed and given to be known in
the Son. We can know it as the love of Christ, but we
see it as such only when we discover behind it the love
of the Father and the Spirit and, in turn, understand the
whole triune love as the origin of the Incarnation of the
Son and of his connection with us.

It is a *love transcending all understanding*. Our understanding remains bound to our powers of comprehension; for
this reason it runs up on all sides against limits that are
set by our human nature. But because the love of Christ,
despite his Incarnation, remains the divine, triune love,
it surpasses every understanding. Whenever we think we
are going to finish understanding something, the love of
the Lord points beyond it, because this love is divine and
is constantly ready to lead on to the Father and to the

Spirit. It is contained to such a degree in the triune God that the omnipotence of God and his eternity, which are both limitless, belong to it in the fullest sense.

That you may be filled with all the fullness of God. This filling occurs when we have understood the love of the Lord so well that we know: it transcends all understanding. This means that we are freed of our limits by God himself in order to partake of the infinity of his plenitude. There will no longer be anything left in us that is still empty and could be filled up. When previously the subject was the dwelling of the Lord in us, the distinction between what was his and what was ours, between the dwelling and the dweller, still seemed possible. Now this distinction has been abolished by love. The love of the Lord, which proves itself greater than our knowledge, lifts away the walls between us and him by the quality it possesses of being ever greater, so that we can in truth participate in the whole plenitude of God. The unity the Son establishes between us and him enables us to partake of the unity he forms in love together with the Father and the Spirit, and in which this plenitude has such a preponderance that our limits no longer count for anything.

The whole prayer that Paul has said since falling on his knees before the Father, which began with an exterior act that was itself already caused by love, ends in a full apotheosis of love. In the rapidity with which the Father sweeps us into his plenitude as we fall down praying, it is as if every concept of time is overcome. Our knowing and planning are taken over in an atemporal instant by God, who secures us participation in his eternity.

3:20–21. *To him, who by the power at work in us can do infinitely more than anything we can ask and conceive, to him be glory in the Church and in Christ Jesus for all ages forever and ever. Amen.*

Once more, in closing, Paul sums up the difference between our understanding and God's, between his power and ours. We can *ask and conceive*, and there will always be a proportion between these two factors. We cannot ask more than we can conceive, and our conceiving is tied to understanding, which resides within the limits of our humanity. Even our highest requests and boldest thoughts remain conditioned by the finitude of our being as men. God, in contrast, can *through the power at work in us do infinitely more than anything* of the sort. This power is that of the Son's love, which is so powerful that he dwells in us himself and bursts our limits as if from within. His power, which derives from the Father, cannot be constrained in our narrow limits. Our limits are none at all for him. His love, even though it has deeply penetrated our humanity, keeps all the infinite attributes of the love and of the power of God. Its infinity triumphs everywhere over our finitudes and thus works far beyond the power of our thoughts and wishes. For a moment it seems to take possession of our thoughts and wishes, but it does this only in order to expand them immediately into the infinite and, by bestowing upon them and leaving in their keeping the character of its own power, to give them the dimensions of God's infinity dwelling in them.

We could perhaps risk the attempt to reach our own limits and in so doing transcend them. We could, by a special exertion, follow a thought until it disappears and in this vanishing thought look beyond our finitude, as it were. Or we could conceive a prayer so bold that it, too, seemed to transcend what we can conceive. But when we compare this attempt at transcending our limits with the way in which God surpasses us, we will immediately realize that the two things are entirely disproportionate. When God surpasses us, it is not as if he simply pushed the limits of our finitude farther beyond their present position or made many things possible for us that were hitherto impossible. Rather, he surpasses us totally and infinitely. He bursts our limits *by the power at work in us*, hence, not from outside, but from within, by implanting faith and love into the midst of our soul, in order to let them expand efficaciously; which means that from the outset he lets them work in our being together with us, so that his operation together with ours becomes in faith a single operation, whose unity God produces in us by his grace. When the power working in us explodes our limits, it does even this together with us, without it being any longer possible to delimit how far our operation reaches and how far God's reaches. The love that draws us into the unity of love does not want to be divided any longer from us. There is thus a synergy of God's power with ours.

To God, who works so far beyond our power, *be glory in the Church and in Christ Jesus*. Christ and the Church belong together. The Church as bride glorifies the bridegroom, and the bridegroom glorifies the bride by making her his bride. It is by means of these two glorifications that the Father is glorified. The love of the Father ceases to make divisions between the Son and the Church; he recognizes in the Church the efficacious power of the incarnate Son. When Paul understands the power at work in us as the power of God, he knows that this power lives simultaneously in the Lord and in the Church, that the Church embodies the power of the Son that is efficacious and operative in us. And we, who form the Church, know and acknowledge it with him and thereby give God the glory.

For all ages forever and ever. Amen. For all present and coming ages, because none of them can subtract itself from this power. Even in this impossibility of evasion there lies a glorification of the power of God, a confession that it effects what it wills, an acknowledgement of its omnipotence. This stands *forever and ever*, because the glorification of God in the Church and in Christ Jesus can suffer no diminution. Once begun, it can only perdure in existence forever, ever further conforming itself to the ever-greater knowledge of love, growing together with it. *Amen.* So be it. Paul has no more intimate desire than the glorification of the triune God in the Son and in the Church. His whole life serves this glorification. He invites the community, and with it all believers, to partake in this glorification.

THE CHURCH

4:1. *Wherefore I admonish you, I, who am a prisoner in the Lord, to walk worthily of the vocation, the portion bestowed upon you.*

Paul admonishes his people on the authority of his calling. He has placed himself at the Lord's service, and it is a part of his office to admonish in the name of the Lord. He admonishes in function of the Lord's will to admonish. The Lord came to love but also to furnish us with admonitions within the context of his love. Paul, who in the foregoing pointed with all his might to the love of the Lord, must now, as a proper servant of this love, follow up with admonitions.

I, who am a prisoner in the Lord. He is in chains for his faith, he can be understood, therefore, as a prisoner for believers and nonbelievers. At the same time he is caught prisoner in his faith. Faith is the preserve, the circle from which he has ceased to step forth and from which alone he can operate. He has made the whole teaching of the Lord his own and, from that point on, can think, speak, and act only in terms of this doctrine.

As a prisoner in chains, he admonishes his people *to walk worthily of their vocation*. For they have to walk. The believer must never stand still. He must walk in the footsteps of the Lord, do his part in the evolution that faith requires and suffer the change that love effects in him. This change must proceed *worthily*, along an approved and appropriate course. But the worthiness derives from the *vocation*, the *portion bestowed upon* those who believe. The Lord calls his own and gives them a calling through this call. The call is one of love of the Lord, and the calling is one of service of this love. Call and calling are mutually conditioned, but because they are of the Lord, they presuppose the worthiness of love. The believer who serves the Lord must do it in a way that is worthy of the Lord; he must never be found outside his service and never outside what is worthy of the Lord. For together with the love of the Lord, he assumes his manner of giving himself and his mind, and a part of this service is that men recognize clearly in faith the trace of the transformation that life in the Lord has wrought. The call of the Lord puts the entire life in requisition, and one of the things that belong to life is activity. One must be able to read from a life whom it serves. The believer lives in responsibility; everything he does must be an answer to the call of the Lord. In Paul this answer is visible even in his imprisonment, but this is not enough; as a prisoner he must admonish others to give their life the mark of the Lord's love.

4:2. *With all humility and gentleness, bearing with one another longanimously in love.*

Humility and gentleness should distinguish believers, because these are properties of the Lord. The Son is humble above all in relation to the Father, because he accepted from him the mission to be man, and his humility is gentle. In relation to us, the Son is above all gentle. Both attributes coincide in him and are expressed in his whole life. We, his servants, who have to reflect his attributes so that everyone may recognize to whom we belong, must be humble and gentle; anything that offended against these attributes would be a breach within our relationship of service. It would then look as if we had taken up with another lord who demanded a different mentality from us.

But Paul knows that we, in order to be humble and gentle, need *longanimity* and patience. It requires a struggle against everything in us that spurs us on against humility and mildness. For as men we incline again and again to set our own goals and norms in the place of the Lord, to fall out of the service of his love. Thus we need longanimity toward ourselves, the longanimity the Lord showed toward us during the whole of his life. But we need it just as well in relation to others, *bearing with one another in love*. In order to bear with one another in service, we absolutely need the love of the Lord, for every one of us, even if he exerts himself to walk in love, falls so easily and so often that the others can bear him only with effort. Thus the commandment of love must be practiced first of all in bearing with our neighbor. The neighbor is here above all the neighbor in faith, the neighbor in service, the neighbor by virtue of one's calling, who is so close to us that we notice everything he does as a man or as one engaged in service. We see his weakness as well as, if not better than, his strength, and in such proximity that longanimity is needed to bear with him. But this entire walk in humility, mildness, and longanimity is possible

only in the love of the Lord, and the Lord, if he lives
in us, lives in us together with his love and places it so
copiously at our disposal that by it we can walk together
with him.

4:3. *Striving with zeal to preserve the unity of the Spirit in
the bond of peace.*

In order to preserve, Christians must strive zealously. For
nothing in this temporal existence keeps itself alive on its
own. They are men exposed to the chances and changes
of human existence, and it is natural for them, not to
be in a steady state of equilibrium, in a conservation of
what has been attained, but rather to change, to reject, or
to lose again what they have once accepted. Sin has un-
derscored this transitoriness even more in human nature.
Everything that perdures and abides, because it partakes
of God's eternity, has become alien to it on account of
the fall. Since then nature has boggled at every repose,
at every equilibrium that has its provenance from God.
If, however, it is to attain such steadfast continuance, this
does not happen without zealous striving, by overcoming
the laws of sinful nature.

The unity of the Spirit is the first thing that must be
preserved. Those who believe partake of the unity of the
Spirit of the triune God. God, who possesses this unity in
full measure, gives them through the Son the possibility
of having a part in it, not only of seeing it, of standing before it, and gazing at it in amazement and perhaps aspiring
to it, but, thanks to the coming of the Son, of truly making it their own, of bringing their spirit to a true unity

with the one Spirit of the triune God. Of welcoming him
in themselves and letting him dwell in them rather than
being in a perpetual conflict with the Spirit of God. But
this unity of spirit between their spirit and the Spirit of
God, precisely because it is of divine origin, can be preserved only through a striving, a zeal, namely, *in the bond
of peace*. Zealous striving is not meant to be like a sort
of battle, an indecisive struggle for the unity that perhaps
appears unattainable. Rather, this striving must be of such
a nature that it regards the perfect end, the unity of the
spirit, as the gift of God already assured him; he submits
himself to it and composes in peace his own disunity so
that he may be steadied by the bond that peace lays upon
him. The peace the Son brings is consequently the opposite of a peace of idleness; it includes zealous striving,
and only thus does it lead to repose. And it is perhaps not
in vain that Paul, before he speaks of this bond of peace,
has spoken of his own bondage for the Lord. He thereby
draws his people into a sort of community with him. Just
as his service has bound him permanently to the Lord,
the service of the community must lay upon it the bond
of peace, in which the restlessness of personal freedoms
comes to rest.

4:4. *One body and one spirit, just as you were also called in
one hope of your calling.*

Paul now takes pains to characterize the unity of the triune God and the unity into which God calls us with
himself so as to make it comprehensible to believers. He
begins with the expression: *one body*. This body, the body

of Christ, which embodies God, which the triune God bestowed upon the Son, has become visible to them in the person of the Lord. They know this body. But in order truly to know it, they must also be apprised of its uniqueness. The triune God has used it in order to redeem man, to reopen to him the way to God; by the body of Christ, by its suffering and dying, but also by its sheer assumption, the Son gave evidence to the Father of his readiness to redeem. He was ready to assume it but also to give it up again for the salvation of the world. As this particular tool, this body is unique and remains so as well through all ages. Whenever the Lord speaks of this body, whenever he lets it become Eucharist: it is the same. Whenever the Church mentions it or lets it assume eucharistic form: it is the same. He allows no possibility of going beyond it or behind it. It is not clothing, but flesh; not similitude, but the thing itself. If the Lord contented himself with this one body in order to operate everything, he thereby hints at the preciousness and holiness of the body. By the fact that the Father created it and the Son was content with this one body, the relative irrepeatable uniqueness of all other bodies becomes manifest.

As the Lord is one body, and as we are one in our bodies, so too there is only one spirit, the Spirit of God, which is at our disposal rather like the one body of Christ. The Spirit, which in the triune God is one from all eternity, in the unity of the Father, of the Son, and of the Holy Spirit, and which is revealed to us as *one* spirit by the triune God. Not, indeed, in a revelation that places us before it, but one that pours itself out into us and surrenders itself to us. As our body comes to share in eternal life through the one body of Christ, so too we cannot be children of God and live in faith except in the one spirit. As soon as our own spirit tried to disengage itself, in order to be self-sufficient as a spirit, it would no longer have the spirit of divine filiation. Because there is only one spirit, the spirit of believers can be filled up and show itself to be a spirit of filiation only if it strives to enter into the unity of this one spirit of God.

Because God wants unity, he calls us also in *one hope* of our *calling*. We are men with a call and a calling. Hence, we stand before God, not as finished, completed beings, but as beings who are connected to him by a relationship based on a call. God does not cease to consider us through his call as men with a call. The call is a reality that envelops our whole life, which most deeply makes us what we are. That we are men with a calling, that we are called at all and can hear the call, presupposes that we are not satisfied with ourselves, that we are not already sated. The ability to hear presupposes a fundamental hope. We hear by hope, and since it is the call more than anything that awakens and forms our hope, we also answer by hope. Both things, call and hope, constitute the mobility of our whole Christian life. If we have once heard the call, it will shape the course of our whole lives. We remain in the call and in the answering of the call.

But the hope to which we have been called is again *one*. We are not called to wildly heterogeneous hopes that would each independently be a splinter of the truth, but to the sole hope that has its unity in the only God and on the basis of which all those called can live within the call. It is this hope that makes a reality the unity of our answer as well as the unity of the conveyance of the call: the hope of God's eternal life. Ultimately, then, something of the unity of God himself, which belongs to the Father, the Son, and the Spirit, but also carries along our creaturely nature. In being offered, in the form of its revelation, this hope possesses the same characteristics of unity as the spirit and as the body of the Lord. They are all goods from God's treasury, which he places at our disposal and which in their unity give evidence of their origin from God. They all have a family resemblance that allows one to recognize their parentage.

4:5. *One Lord, one faith, one baptism.*

One Lord: the God who became visible, who abode among us as man. Paul underscores his unity, so that none of the believers may delude himself and believe that the one Lord could be replaced in ages to come by another or that a second or third God-man could appear alongside him. The oneness of the Son is grounded from all eternity in the Father; and in every promise of the Old Covenant, whatever its terms might have been, the Son was always praised as the one. If the Lord is already one in himself —one in his body, one in his sonship, one in his life of revelation, one in his abiding among us—he is also one in *faith:* he brings us his one Christian faith. This faith is so greatly one in the triune God that every attempt to dissect it, to tear pieces of it from its context, or to refuse parts of it as inessential destroys the whole of it. Only in its unity is the Christian faith true. Every attempt to splinter it or to reinterpret it in another sense robs it of the truth of its unity, ruins it utterly. Faith is, after all, the expression in us of the triune God and, therefore, most perfect unity. If the faith were no longer one in us, God himself would no longer need to be one in us. The unity of the triune God grounds in us the unity of faith. Like faith, the sacraments, too, are one. *One baptism.* Whether the Lord dispensed it or whether it was his disciples and priests: they all baptize in the one Spirit, who brings the one faith. Thus the sense for the unity of God is planted in us thanks to the unity of baptism. The multiplicity of baptisms and of recipients of baptism only underscores this unity. Before baptism, man possesses a life that does not aspire to unity; he has his own opinion and is satisfied within his own limits. As soon as he is baptized, he becomes a bearer of the one truth and strives with all his might to enter into this unity. This does not signify any narrowing or impoverishment of multiplicity, for this unity is that of the God who encompasses all things. Therefore, the more we penetrate into truth, the ampler and more variegated it becomes and enriches us by catholically expanding our spirit.

4:6. One God and Father of all, who is above all and through all and in all.

The unity of God to which Paul reverts is the condition and explanation of the unity of the Son, of faith, and of baptism. God has conferred upon all that is his the property of oneness. This one God is the Father of all, not only because he created all, but because, as Father of the Son, he gave the Son all as brothers. As a consequence of

the redemption, he received in a new way the property
of fatherhood; this is not a secondary fatherhood subordinated to the first, but the proper and essential paternity
grounded in the divine intention and decree, for whose
sake he had formerly established the first.

This Father is above all, because he is God and eternally
Father and because, as his creatures, we stand under him,
since no creature can be commensurate with him. He is
above us by virtue of his being God, by virtue of every
one of his revelations, by virtue of the one faith, the one
baptism, and the one Son. His being *above all* does not
mean that he is removed from us but chiefly signifies the
visible manifestation of his eternal summons, in which he
invites us to return to him in a constant upward movement toward himself, in an upward striving that his grace
makes possible without lessening in any degree his being
above us. But the Father is also *through all*; through the
Son he is in a permanent state of being communicated in
our midst. The Son, who came in order to glorify him,
brings him to us without any rupture of continuity; but
by showing us as man how to glorify the Father, he gives
to every believer the possibility of sharing in this glorification and consequently of sharing in his mediation. The
through all retains this twofold meaning, in which at first
the Son alone is the mediator of the Father, and then we
become partakers of this mediation. And *in all*: he has
chosen all in order to be in all. He is not in some individuals so as to be more fully represented in them the less
he is represented in others. His being Father of all exists
in a unity with his being in all. He wants to be in each of
his children just as he was in his Son, and he wants to be

in us in a living way. This vitality is the answer he gives
to himself in us, in order that he may be the Father of all.
When we allow the Father to be in us, we acknowledge
that we are his children and live in this unity with him
and the Son and the Spirit.

4:7. *But to each one of us grace has been given according to the*
measure of the donation of Christ.

All along the Father had wanted to give his *grace* to all
who were his. But in the Old Covenant it was not yet
evident how great the gift was that was to be the portion
of each one of them. Paul now makes known that the
donation has a measure, that it is possible to measure the
share of each one. And that the measure lies in the *dona-*
tion of Christ, which the Lord proclaims by his Incarnation, exhibits ever more plainly in the course of his life,
and fulfills by means of his Cross. His whole existence
is donation, both for the Father and for men; every act it
contains, every prayer, every word, every miracle, every
intention, and every realization in act: everything is an
expression of this gift. The Lord is engaged in a perennial
act of giving. Now there is a ratio between this act of giving and the grace apportioned to us. The measure of the
donation is taken as the measure of the grace assigned to
us. So that from the very outset grace always stands in the
light of the Son's donation, always remains connected to
him, and we can perceive the signs of the Son's donation
in everything we receive. For the Christian there is no
casual, random grace; nor is there any grace in isolation
either. All grace hangs together coherently with the dona-

tion of the Son and retains this coherence in its intention, in its actual unfolding, and in its effect; without a break in continuity, it draws its entire life from the Son. We can never perfectly survey the measure that is thus applied, inasmuch as even the love of the Son itself surpasses all understanding; yet we do understand this much: grace itself partakes of the Lord's property of being greater and more; hence, in us too, it is more than we can measure. This grace is for the benefit *of each one of us*; it is inherent in faith and disseminates itself, multiplies itself, and lives in the believer from the moment he says Yes to faith.

4:8. *Therefore it is written: ascending on high he has taken captivity captive, giving gifts to men.*

Paul supports himself with a statement of the Old Covenant. He wants to show the unity of promise and realization, even in relation to the gifts of the Lord. What is surprising in the Lord should always reside in the fact that he is ever greater, not in an outward impression of precipitation and suddenness. We are such as have been prepared by the Old Covenant and are expecting something. The fulfillment of God comes as an answer. It satisfies a longing that it had itself awakened in the Old Covenant, but it satisfies in God's manner: by bringing infinitely more than what could have been expected.

Ascending on high. That means to heaven, in a return movement to the Father. When the Son descended to earth, he was alone, accompanied only by the Father and by the Holy Spirit, who laid him in the womb of the Mother. These companions were invisible when he came forth as man, inasmuch as they did not become man together with him. In an invisible manner he bore from the very beginning men's *captivity*, the sin of the world. He had already borne it from eternity, insofar as from eternity he had declared himself ready to take it upon himself if the Father wanted to send him. But in eternity it did not yet have the weight it now has, when he is alone on earth as man and at the end is abandoned by the Father on the Cross. When, ascending on high, he returns to the Father, he takes captivity *captive*; he takes it back with him and by this means releases men from their captivity to sin. He takes with him into heaven what in a certain sense he had already had beforehand in heaven but which had not yet become a reality in the world as long as the Cross had not yet been suffered through. On the Cross he bore in full truth the burden he had previously borne in the form of promise, and he takes it with himself as a discharged burden, so that men may pass from being sinners to being his liberated brothers.

In so doing he *gave gifts to men*, presents of grace that could not be distributed to them as long as they were ensnared and held captive in their sin, impeded in their freedom, unable to receive. Liberated from sin, they are free and possess in full measure the possibility of receiving what the Lord wants to give them: the whole gift of his life, which is established in the grace of the Father.

4:9. But what does "He has ascended" mean except that he also descended first into the lower regions of the earth?

Paul now connects the Lord's Ascension to his descent into hell, and in such a way that it ought to become evident how the two things stand in a relationship of absolute mutual dependence. In becoming man, the Lord took upon himself, not only the burden of those sins that were committed during his earthly life, but the burden of all sins. For this reason his Incarnation was also necessarily tied to his journeying to a place where all the sins of the world, both past and present, are gathered, hence to *his also descending first into the lower regions of the earth*, to the realm where the light of grace no longer shines, where there is no sign of grace to be found, where the dwelling of the triune God is not only rejected but rendered impossible. He descended into hell, once again in solitude, in order to do there the last thing still required by the deed of the Cross: to gather everything that in a certain sense he had not met with during his earthly life. It was there that he loaded upon himself the final burdens that at last were to make possible his return to the Father, as if his ascent were dependent upon his descent, as if he had had no possibility of returning into heaven before going down into hell. This voyage down below hangs together seamlessly with the gifts he distributes to men on going up; his act of bearing transforms the burden of sin into a burden of grace.

Perhaps men had, so long as he sojourned among them, grown somewhat accustomed to his human appearance, and it was not always entirely obvious to them what a

mass of sins he actually had weighing upon him. Perhaps
they confused a bit his everyday life with their own and
thought that even a God could live quite comfortably
on earth. The cross appeared then as a great suffering
indeed, but, for all that, as a separate deed in this human life, which, moreover, did not look like a bearing of
sins. But when Paul now explains that the descent is the
necessary prerequisite for the ascent, he shows that the
Lord aimed toward this descent all along, that he spent
his whole life in view of and in the foreknowledge of this
descent. Whenever he thought of the Father and of his
return to him, he also saw that the way to realizing this
reunion had to pass right through the descent into hell.
For only thus could he give the work of redemption its
full extension.

4:10. *The one who descended is also the very one who ascended
above all the heavens in order to fill up all things.*

In this identity of the Lord there resides not only his
unity as redeemer who descends to discharge his most
difficult duty and who ascends to become a partaker of
the highest joy; but his whole life as God from eternity
and his whole life as man among us are also included in
it. He is always the same, always of the same nature, of
the same character, of the same power and potentiality.
As the one descending from heaven to earth, from earth
to the Cross, from the Cross to hell, he was always the
same person he has been from eternity in heaven. He
does not need to expropriate himself of his essence and
character in order to live for a while in time. As man,

he is not a modified God, and, as God, he is no altered man. He is fullness in person: God and man, and both in a perfect, immutable manner.

He who descends, as if in order to take upon himself the uttermost sins, *is also the very one who ascended*, who returns in joy to the Father. But in everything he does, he has this one goal: he intends to *fill up all things*. This means, not only to bear and cancel the entire burden of sin, but to give to the Father and to the Spirit and to all believers the whole plenitude. He fills up all things; he fulfills every promise and prophecy that has been given to men from the beginning, the whole promise of the redemption of the world just as it had been planned in the Father's design; and in returning to the Father, he also fulfills his perennial, definitive abode among us. This fulfillment contains the gift of the Eucharist as well as the fulfillment of our faith, of our being in the triune God and—in regard to us—the fulfillment of his eternal life in the presence of the Father. In himself the Son was eternally filled, but after his Incarnation, he is for us and in us as well. It is like the case of a man whom another, unbeknown to him, has devoted his whole life to provide and struggle for and who only much later, when he learns of this other man's love, discovers that everything that seemed incomprehensible to him was a labor of love: "So it was this man whom I have to thank for everything!" He reviews all the particulars of his existence and discovers everywhere the traces of that solicitous love. Or it is similar to a food that has an excellent taste; one inquires into the reasons and discovers from the recipe how many ingredients and how much work was necessary to produce this simple taste. The Christian can contemplate in faith his life and the world in this way, and his analysis will eventually turn up the fullness of the Lord, which is spread everywhere and which is interwoven with everything. There is nothing on earth or in heaven, or in the underworld, that has not been touched by his Incarnation or that has not undergone perfect fulfillment thanks to his return to the Father. From now on everything is drawn into the unity of the Lord, the unity he has possessed forever in the Father and in the Spirit, but which, in fulfilling every promise, he now gives to us, so that we may live in it together with the triune God.

4:11. *And he has made some apostles and others prophets, others evangelists, others shepherds and teachers.*

Ascending to the Father, the Son distributes his gifts, which he publicly unveils at the very moment of his return into heaven. Previously they were, so to say, concealed on his person; now they are ready to be distributed. The Father must receive the assurance upon his return that his work remains alive. That what was begun out of love for the Father is not interrupted by this return. That the Son is convinced that, even without being visible, he can go on working and may place a part of his work in the hands of believers without thereby jeopardizing it. So the distribution of gifts becomes the filling of offices in the Lord's work.

Paul begins by naming *apostles* and *prophets*. The prophets belong in part to the New Covenant—there will again and again be such prophets—and partly, in our eyes, to the Old Covenant; they announced the promise without witnessing the fulfillment themselves. Yet upon his return to the Father, the Son also installs prophets; that is, he gives them the realization of the promise in the final fulfillment of his Incarnation, which we are privileged to witness. He does not leave them behind him, in a state of having fallen short, but on his return also fulfills their mission, as he does everything else. He suspends in a certain sense their temporality in order to give them within the eternal truth the additional gift of temporality of the New Covenant, with the aim of bringing the Old and New Covenants to a unity in them. Like them, all those who have a mission also receive their fulfillment from this source. The apostles possessed, so long as the Lord abode on earth, a mission that was wholly enclosed within the Lord's earthly mission. He sent them out on a trial basis to preach and to perform other commissions, but on the condition that they always came back in order to render an account and to receive new commissions. Only when the Lord returns to the Father does he leave his mission in their charge as an independent one, thus appointing them definitively as apostles. Before, they were representatives of the visible Lord, and their task was to bring his visibility to the attention of men. Now they are administrators of his total, heavenly mission and have to pledge their total existence for it.

Others evangelists. He appoints a few of his disciples, who lived with him or else knew about him, who received his doctrine, while always comprehending it in a purely subjective fashion, to recount his earthly existence. He endows them with that inspiration in virtue of which they are able to report everything in an objective truth. What they will now state concerning him, his life, and his words is not going to be mere personal reminiscence but will be included within the truth of revelation coming from heaven.

Others shepherds and teachers. The pastors have to direct the Lord's sheep, give them what the Lord gave them, lead them, help them, assemble them, keep them from going astray, and their disposition in doing so has to be that of solicitude for souls. While the teachers are charged with transmitting doctrine and keeping it pure, the pastors have the office of assisting to translate doctrine into Christian action. The entire truth of the Lord is entrusted to the teachers in the sense that they have to proclaim it in his name. In their proclamation, they must remain within this truth and are not permitted to strike out anything from its content.

The Lord distributes in this way the totality of his mission and indicates within it certain areas of competence that he entrusts to the administration of individuals. He showed them how these areas are to be administered while he was among them on earth. Now he gives these areas to them in freedom, not, however, by separating himself from them, but by taking them into his return to the Father. They are those whom the Lord brings back with him to the Father and who, precisely in this way, are permitted to experience the grace of the mission. The Lord is from now on withdrawn from their sight, but he gives them the inner assurance of his abiding among them in that he leaves in their charge his entire mission.

When he returns to the Father, he brings his mission

in the state of consummation. But in letting the disciples partake of it just now, he demonstrates that he leaves it in their charge at the moment when it *is* being completed. As if they were being allowed to help put the finishing touches on it.

4:12. *In order to equip the saints for the work of ministry, in order to build up the body of Christ.*

All of this does not happen so that the disciples may attain their own perfection; rather, it is just as urgent that this mission radiate outward in action when they receive it as when the Lord carried it. None of these men overwhelmed with gifts receives them for himself; all gifts are intended to be passed on. They are given to *equip the saints*, and those who believe must submit to this equipping. It is part of their faith, which they have likewise not received for themselves alone, since it is meant to be *one* faith in all. If the Son assumed man's nature in order to give up his life, this taking and giving continues to exist in his teaching and is transmitted by the apostles and prophets, evangelists, shepherds, and teachers to the other believers *for the work of ministry*. Service of the Lord is, so to say, included within a work that transcends the individual. No one serves for himself alone. His service must take into account the service of others. There is such a thing as believing together, shouldering the burden together, serving together. There is a sort of infection of service. The entirety of service constitutes a work; a work of faith, of love of neighbor, of mission. It is as if all those sent with a mission had to work together to

realize the whole service of the Lord, each one in his direction, each one fulfilling his determinate task, but everyone connected to everyone else and everyone partici-
pating in the indivisible commission of the Lord. Hence,
no disunity is possible either in service or in the diverse
gifts, and the unity of the truth is preserved intact. So
Paul repeats here with a practical twist the initial teaching
of the chapter.

In order to build up the body of Christ. It is precisely in the
return to the Father, at which time the Lord disappears
bodily, that he entrusts his body to be built up by his
own. He gives it to the Church, and thanks to this gift
the Church, his bride, becomes his body. This body must,
in order to remain living, be continually built up anew.
Its continued existence depends upon the ceaseless cooperation of all believers. It is like a vessel whose content
is the life of every believer. If it were not permanently
being built up, it would collapse, and those equipped for
the work of ministry would have proved themselves unworthy of the grace of belonging to the body of Christ
on earth.

The Church, then, undertakes now the edification of
the body of Christ. It would not be enough for the Lord
to leave his spiritual mission to the charge of his own; he
gives it to them incarnated in his body. He commits this
body as a whole to the whole Church and at the same
time entrusts it to her in the always irrepeatable uniqueness of the Eucharist, yet in such a way that the two retain
their vitality only together and by means of each other:
no Eucharist without Church; no Church without Eucharist. He who receives the Eucharist receives the life

of the Lord, so that he must thereby become a prop of the Church, that the energy he has received might enter efficaciously into the Church, for the building up of the body of Christ in the Church.

The body of Christ that returns to the Father is at that moment, so to say, at its maximum potency. It can be given, distributed, multiplied, eternalized, both in the Eucharist as well as in the body of the Church. She is his body as the expression and bearer of his spirit, of his intentions, of his essence. She is so in virtue of the offices and missions, which are like his organs in which his spirit acquires concrete reality. The Eucharist is the bearer more of his being than of his character; the Church is the bearer more of his essence than of his being. Just as an essence, in order to be able to deploy itself and to perform its mission, needs an interior stimulus, the Church possesses at her center the Eucharist. It is like a stake fixed in her middle, immovably, that prevents the Church from distancing herself from this essence and that sets forth this essence as a reality.

And all this at the moment of the return to the Father, when the Lord has just disappeared from his own. Just as the survivors suddenly understand the deceased better when they open his will, when they read through his papers, which cast a different light on his whole life and supplement it. It is no longer possible to speak with him about these things; one must now grow into the greater, more objective image of him.

4:13. *Until we have all attained to the unity of faith and know-*
ledge of the Son of God, to a perfect man, to the measure of the
maturity of the fullness of Christ.

Everything the Lord instituted is in a "toward". Everything is aimed at our development, which, however, is not
without a law; it is a development that the Lord not only
requires but to which he lends himself as a criterion of
fullness, as an example of perfection. It will reach its end
only when we have attained what the Lord showed us in
himself as our exemplar. Until then we remain within the
laws of mediation and hierarchy that are now in force. In
his distribution of charisms, the Lord immediately erected
a whole structure, issued strict guidelines, regulated the
possibilities of development in all directions. No one must
be left without support and direction within the personal
evolution taking place in him. However this evolution
may run its course, it will always have the Lord as measure and will always finish in the Lord. It is not as individuals that we are to attain to him but *all* together. The
goal is chiefly the *unity of faith and knowledge of the Son of*
God. Faith is the perfect unity, and every partial aspect of
faith leads back into its unity. The part can be brought
into relief only for a moment in order to display its full
content more plainly, but, in so doing, it will throw a
clearer light not only on itself but on the whole faith; it
will become evident how every individual aspect down
to the smallest detail is provided for and indispensable in
the unity of faith. This unity of faith is also at the basis of
the unity of the knowledge of the Son of God, who, in
being recognized as the Son, shows the Father in the Holy

Spirit and thus the primordial source of unity. The more
the knowledge of the Son deepens and expands, the closer
the Father comes to us; the knowledge of both grows together. We are permitted to set off particulars about the
Son as well in order to contemplate them closer at hand,
but only in such a way that they finally lead us back again
to deepened contemplation of the unity of the Son and,
through him, of the Trinity. Whatever one can come to
know about the Son will always serve to make clear what
is proper to the triune God. And this knowledge of the
Son mediates the integral faith: the Son himself lives out
undivided unity as our exemplar, in that through all his
words, deeds, and wonders he refers to this undivided
unity. This unity is already implicit in the statement that
he came in order to glorify the Father, for he lives in
the strict logic of his coming. Everything he does can be
explained and understood under the heading of glorification of the Father and can be reduced to it. But the glorification consists in his bringing back the creation, and us
in it, to the Father. Thus he gathers us everywhere into
unity, which remains indivisible: in him, in the Father,
in the integral faith. Returning into this unity, we have
the duty to put our own contribution into it.

But we cannot return as the sinners we were but only
as the redeemed of the Lord. We must therefore grow
into his own redemptive work, accepting from him *his
measure. We must become a perfect man.* Before the Son appeared, we could claim that we did not know the perfect end. We could say perhaps that we tried to do our
best but did not know how to do it. The Son, during
his stay among us, showed us the nature of the perfect

man, and did it with such force that it is impossible not to understand him. That we must keep before our eyes his action and thought in all our action and thought. We are now able to live according to his measure: before him and in him at the same time, because living before him includes the knowledge that he lives in us. We cannot behold him without in turn being beheld and therefore knowing that he came in order to save us and to live in us. This knowledge is already a part of his one truth and a part of the grace of faith that is developing in us.

To the measure of the maturity of the fullness of Christ. Our faith gives us a measure. It cannot unfold in one direction while our life aims in another. Our life must become an expression of faith. It can do this only if it subordinates itself to this faith, if it discovers in it the law of the unity of life. Now, the perfect *plenitude* was given to the Lord his whole life long: the knowledge of the Father, the knowledge about his own divinity, the comprehensive vision of his own mission, the entire life framed by the Incarnation within the will of the Father were always completely present in his mind. We, on the other hand, with our slow development, our hesitant understanding, cannot become partakers of the perfect fullness, as it is represented by the *maturity* of the man, without a long process of maturation. Its goal lies for us in the Lord's age of adulthood, and our maturation must lead us to that point. According to the Apostle, we can attain it through the unity of faith and of the knowledge of the Son. But in our consciousness, we will never have arrived but will constantly remain in the phase of maturation. Along the way, however, the Lord gives himself to us in such an abundance and clarity that we will not be tempted to be perpetually fixated on the distance that separates us from him. We will keep him before our eyes as the perfect measure, and, if we do not turn our gaze from him, our whole process of maturation to unity will be accomplished in the presence of the maturity and fullness of the Lord.

4:14. *So that we may no longer be immature children, rocked and tossed about by every wind of doctrine, deceived by men, misled by craft into error.*

We must be grown up and comport ourselves as adults. And we have to do so in virtue of the knowledge of faith and the knowledge of the Son. This unity of the two, which lives in the triune God, is conveyed to us by the Spirit and presented as an exemplar in the life of the Incarnate One. The Lord never wavered as man among us men in his unity with the Father and the Spirit. He never lost the perfect certainty of his mission. In order to be able to bring us back to the Father as belonging to him, he must require the same certainty of us. But he does not wait while we develop to adulthood; he makes the possibility of being adults part of the gift he bestows upon us on our way back to the Father. He has bequeathed to us a firm guide, not only insofar as he has made accessible to us his unity with the Father, his faith, but also in having given us in these gifts a solid structure, a course of development. For this reason, in our striving toward unity we also have the certainty that we can arrive at the goal, that the process of growing up, indeed, the state of adulthood in him, is no far-off utopia but an immediate reality.

If we remained immature children, we would be *rocked and tossed about by every wind of doctrine.* Everything that came our way with a power of attraction could fling us off course and off balance. As human beings, we are subject to the laws of nature, from which we are ultimately exempted as believers by the unity of faith, because in faith we possess a supernatural point of equilibrium and can pursue and lead back into unity everything that moves us. As men, we remain susceptible to every alteration, every opinion, every new desire. Because this is our nature as human beings, we have a tendency to consider even doctrine as if it were subject to the same processes of evolution and transformation. But in accord with the requirement of adulthood, we will, despite the continuing impressionability for new, hitherto unnoticed aspects of the faith, always immediately have the desire to verify them in the light of unity and to accept them only when they are an expression and portion of this unity. If this is not the case, we are not deeply stirred by them, we are not tossed about; they leave us neither hot nor cold. The *deceit of men* will not trouble us. We will take cognizance of it, but we will have done with it. In the unity of faith, the Lord has given us an infallible rule of thumb: every time something moves and pulls us, we need only attend to whether the end of the string is in the Lord's hands. For everything depends on the end. The deception of men does not come out all at once and in a grossly evident way but often *misleads by craft into error.* Even those who do not live in God and in the unity of faith aspire in their life to a unity that in their eyes would be attained if as many other people as possible shared their way of seeing things. Thus they cannot let believers alone, they try to win them over, and it is often not so easy to tell the difference between their arguments and those of faith. They can adduce many persuasive reasons and can mislead even believers who are not on guard. But in the unity of faith and of knowledge of the Son of God, God has given those who wish to be adults an infallible means to keep themselves in the truth. The trial of subtle craft and cunning will not have to lead to an extreme rocking and tossing about, will not make adults appear as children, and will not betray believers to deception.

4:15. *But rather, holding firm the truth in love, may grow in every respect up to him who is the head, Christ.*

To hold firm the truth in love means not to divorce truth from love. If a serious separation were possible, truth and love would not belong to unity, which means that when all is said and done they could not be Christian. Thanks to the gifts the Lord has bestowed upon us, we can unite truth and love in ourselves; for we know that both exist in him and through him lead back to the Father. If we were immature children, we could hold firm neither truth nor love, we would always have to be setting off in search of them, and it would be quite possible for us to resolve to hold firm as definitive a truth that was not comprised in love or to consider as love something that was not contained in the truth. In virtue of the requirement of adulthood, we are capable of holding firm this unity, in such a way that it grows to maturity together with us; the farther we progress, the firmer our hold of them becomes and the better we know both love and truth. The two things bind us more and more, and this obligation in turn means growth in both toward unity. It is impossible for one to develop in us at the expense of the other. To pursue the truth without growing in love, to love without directing oneself according to the truth, would signify a violent rupture of unity, hurling oneself out of unity. But as we hold unity firm, we will *grow up in every respect*, by the force of truth and love, and, consequently, through the unity that the Lord bestows upon us, which strikes root in us and, as it grows, takes possession of us and causes us to grow together with it into a unity that becomes ever greater. *Toward him who is the head, Christ.* The Lord is always unity, even though on earth he is this seemingly isolated, exposed man. We individual men cannot grow into unity otherwise than in him who is the head. He himself invites us to grow in him as his members. He wants by these means to overcome even the seeming distance of the members from the head, their apparent autonomy; to make us grow so much *in every respect* in him that the Father can no longer see us in any respect outside the Son but can distinguish us only by beholding us in the Son, in that place which the Son assigned to us in himself. In a perfect unity with the Son, who leads us back into this unity through his perfect unity with the Father and the Spirit.

4:16. *From him the whole body, held together and forming a solid structure through mutually supporting articulations, according to the operative power meted out to each individual, accomplishes the growth of the body for its own edification.*

From the Lord the whole body receives its strength, its efficacy and its growth, with the result that no believer could ever fulfill the requirement to grow without the assistance of the Lord. But as the source of the body's growth and compact structure, the Lord serves not only the individual but all the saints, the entirety of his people on earth, the Church. He gives it the life that, as the Incarnate One, he received from the Father, which he pours out on the Cross in order to be perennially able to place it at the disposal of all those who belong to him. Here he becomes the inexhaustible spring of life that flows without ceasing, so much so that no body, whether the personal body of believers or the body of the Church, is at all conceivable without him. This body is *held together* and forms a *solid structure.* Its unity is not sameness of kind: it is so constituted that, while every member grows and lives according to the efficacious activity demanded of him, he can reach his personal unity only *through mutually supporting articulations.* Here the body becomes an image of faith, of the unity, and of the organization of faith in the knowledge of the Son. The single parts and members are, of course, visible and operative, but only on the strength of the mutual support of all the articulations. The unity of the whole as well as that of the parts persists only when all members work together as functions of the whole. Every part allows the other to be comprehensible, and each one lives only so long as the other lives along with it. No life is possible in the singular, but only in that unity that by its organization reveals itself to be living unity. All life is a being together, a growing together, and a serving together. Its unity is mediated by the life of the Lord, by his own unity, which he makes available and which is infused into every member. It is not a unity in the singular but living unity in God with the Father and the Spirit. Through this bestowing of life, two bodies come into being as the one body of the Lord: the body of the individual believer, which is a function in the Church, and the body of the Church. *According to the operative power meted out to each one,* according to the distributions of the Lord's charisms, which are certainly guided to some extent by the needs and capabilities of the individuals in question, but above and beyond that are governed by the needs of the body as a whole, which transcend these individuals. No more than all the members of the body will be hands could all believers think of becoming teachers of the Church, because the functions always have to be determined according to the needs indicated by the Lord. *For its own edification in love.* This is the purpose that growth serves. When the Lord gives himself to us as the consummated man, into whom we will have to mature and grow, then he gives us the measure of the attainable. As it were, the form, the vessel, into which our body has to grow as its contents. This growth can take place only in love. We cannot understand the reciprocal services of the members without love; they are wholly functions of the love that in the body is one with truth.

So they have truth only to the extent that they forego their own edification in order to consecrate themselves to the service of the building up of the whole body in love.

THE LIFE OF CHRISTIANS

4:17. *This, then, I say and testify in the Lord: you must no longer walk as do the Gentiles, in the vanity of their mind.*

Paul *says* this. He speaks, not of himself, but *in the Lord*. And his declaration is further strengthened by the fact that he also *testifies* to it in the Lord. It is of great consequence to him that precisely this statement be understood by the community as fully valid. Every statement of the believer is fully valid to the extent that it is spoken in faith, originates from the unity of faith, and is thereby brought forth in that unity with the Lord himself that faith produces between the believer and the Lord, inasmuch as it involves everything the believer does, including, therefore, his spoken word. He gives this word a corroborating sanction that comes from the Word of God, because by reason of faith this word cannot stand in any contradiction to or distance from the Word pronounced by God.

And the momentous word is: *You must no longer walk as do the Gentiles*. Both walk, since they are men, but the walk of believers is directed by the Lord. He gives them the way and accompanies them upon it, because he is himself the way. The Gentiles, in contrast, build for themselves their own way, *in the vanity of their mind*. On the way that they walk, they can mark stretches and points, plot out cross-sections; they can determine where they have stood and where they now stand. But the way as a whole does not proceed in the Lord but in themselves, in the vanity of their mind. It is vain, because it has themselves both as subject and as object. They set out from themselves in order to return to themselves with that much more security. Their *mind* comprises every sensible perception, every intention, and every thought of their own. The stages along this way, in however great a number they may trace them out, are all locked within their own desire, within their own ego. For this reason there is at bottom no progress here, no transcendence of one's own ego, no distance from the point of departure; everything spins to the very last within the circle of their subjectivity. The distance from the ego remains constant, and since it is determined by vanity, it equals zero and stays at point zero.

4:18. *They are darkened in their intelligence, alienated from the life of God by the ignorance that is in them because of the hardening of their hearts.*

When God created man, he gave him an intelligence of his own, which was living and capable of development. An intelligence that both leads men and is ruled by them at the same time, in a relationship of reciprocal possession. There exists between man and his intelligence a lively back and forth, an interplay. Intelligence thus lives in a unity with man, with his life, and this unity is founded in God. For God did not leave Adam exposed but created him to be in perfect communication and inseparable communion of life with himself. The life of God fills up

the life and intelligence of man in union, gives vitality
to his life, clears his intelligence, and allows him to walk
in God. It is for this reason that the intelligence of the
Gentiles is *darkened*, because they are *alienated from the life
of God*. The communication that would allow their intelligence to remain lively and clear as God intends it to
be is cut off; the influx of divine life is dried up. Their
intelligence thus goes to ruin. It now has to rely upon
man alone; it no longer draws from outside the materials
and stimuli needed for its further development. In this
way the alienation goes on increasing *because of the ignorance that is in them*. By their refusal to remain in contact with God's life, they pronounced their own death
sentence, which, moreover, was immediately executed in
such a way that every memory, every knowledge is extinguished, and they end up by falling subject to a complete
ignorance in all things concerning God. This ignorance,
however, does not remain purely intellectual but runs parallel to the *hardening of their hearts*. They become inaccessible to love and truth. Nothing that is not founded in
their own ego reaches them any more. The more igno-
rant they become, the more hardened as well, so that even
their searching ceases, their nostalgia is extinguished, and
they are increasingly satisfied with themselves and end up
totally losing every feeling for the closeness of God and
the atmosphere of faith. In the end, they live in a world
completely separated from the world of God. What comes
from God no longer reaches them, and they themselves
are not aware of any sort of longing to break out of their
darkness.

4:19. *They have become without feeling and have delivered themselves over to debauchery, in order to perpetrate every impurity in covetousness.*

The feeling of which Paul speaks here can continue to exist only in contact with God. But since the Gentiles have lost every contact with him, this feeling has disappeared as well: the sensitivity to good and evil in the sense of what God wills and rejects, the sense for a life within the will and life of God. Since they no longer have this wealth, the feeling of faith that was God's gift to them, and yet possess a soul and must live as men, they have to produce a substitute for themselves. They must bind in a new relationship everything in them that God had reserved to himself. Since they know only themselves, they must bind everything to themselves. Return to themselves also with their feeling and place themselves in the center as its felt object. They have thus *delivered themselves over to debauchery*, that is, to the lawlessness of sensuality that is no longer considered and used as a gift of God but is used in itself, is intensified in itself, and knows as its only goal its own self-bound pleasure. Thus they have perpetrated *every impurity*; they have not failed to experience every possible employment of their drives and senses that they could discover. They have used their intelligence, whose contact with God is now choked off, to augment their own possession in every conceivable manner, always in connection with *covetousness*. A covetousness that is rooted in their pleasure, which, therefore, extends just as much to interior impure pleasure as to exterior goods and which of itself knows no limit:

they have greedily amassed everything transitory in order to count as rich and full, at least in their own eyes. All this in turn has only alienated them more and more from God, so that it now seems there is no hope of hooking them in some spot in order to reel them round to another way of thinking. Wherever God's law was, they have set up laws of their own and are therefore convinced of the possibility of an independent life. Each one has tried to find in himself a unity that is self-sufficient and has no need of God.

4:20. *You, on the other hand, did not learn Christ in this way.*

Paul sharply divides off his own people from the unbelievers. He knows that the former have learned the Lord, that they have received him together with his being and his doctrine, so that he lives in them and develops as if out of them. Their reception of the Lord would be comparable to the acceptance of a drug in a body. The drug works, develops its capabilities by transforming and stimulating everything in the body with which it comes in contact. Learning the Lord has such a decisive effect on man that from now on the Lord is to be known for the believer in virtue of faith. The Gentiles also learn, receive knowledge and skills from others, and develop themselves, but these things have nothing in common with what faith teaches the believer, so that, for everyone who believes, and in some sense even for everyone who does not believe, the two curricula can be kept clearly apart. The Gentile stands above what he has learned, because he has turned it into a function of himself. He learns it in order to be able to dispose of it. The Christian stands under and within what he has learned. It is like a covering and a roof for him. He knows that what he has learned is greater than he himself, and he is thankful to find it both above him and around him. He does not want what he has learned to serve him; he wants to be in its service. Everything with the Gentiles leads to their self-enrichment; everything they learn becomes a serviceable tool for their pleasure and satisfaction. This can be connected with a great deal of ethics and religious thoughts; it does not keep the deepest thought from being that of their own welfare. The ultimate thought of the Christian, on the other hand, is the service of the Lord.

4:21–22. *If indeed you have heard of him and were instructed in him, as it befits the truth in Christ Jesus, considering your former conduct, rid yourselves of the old man, who perishes according to deceitful pleasures.*

It is clear that the believers have heard of the Lord, indeed, are bound by what they have heard. Their faith and their having heard form a unity, and they live by it. This unity binds them not only to the Lord but also to the Apostle; it gives him the right to admonish them and obliges them to listen to his admonition and to live according to it. For everything they have heard of the Lord is meant to be received into their life, until it becomes wholly an expression of what they have heard. It is thereby distinguished from their earlier conduct, which was the same as that of the Gentiles. The division between Christians and Gentiles, Christian conduct and Gentile conduct is complete. It is not possible for Christians to synthesize the two or to hit on a compromise between them. What they have heard of the Lord, which is what they are instructed in, is not only perfect in itself but is also enough for them. It suffices objectively, and it is sufficient subjectively as well in the sense that the hearing and the instruction have been sufficient. The Lord did not elucidate certain points of his teaching while leaving others obscure, so that those who believe would be forced to seek supplements elsewhere, for example, among the Gentiles. Rather, the teaching and instruction of the Lord are sufficient for all aspects of their life. *As it befits the truth in Christ Jesus.* What they have learned has become truth for them through the Lord, because it had already been truth in him first in his unity with the Father and the Spirit. The truth, which is one and the same, is only translated and applied otherwise in man than in God. They must *rid themselves of the old man*, which the Lord does not need to do. But if he invites them to share his life with him, to apprehend his perfect truth, a break with their past is necessarily involved, because our old sinful man would not be capable of this life and of this truth. If the old man were not overcome, man would be cleaved into two subjects, one old and the other new, and it is precisely this cleavage that the Lord's teaching would not tolerate. For the Lord wills to see in us the sort of man he can bring back into the unity of the Father.

The old man *perishes,* while the new man enters into new life with the Lord, is liberated by the Lord in the unity of faith and truth from everything that can perish, and finally enters into eternal life. The old man was perishing on account of *deceitful pleasures*; pleasures that originally lay rooted in his nature as concupiscible powers but were exploited and intensified by the inclination to sin; pleasures that became deceitful because they alienated him more and more from God and from eternal life. The new man takes advantage of everything to place it into the unity of the Lord. Everything that in itself is transitory in man is saved by being brought into the imperishable unity of God, not only by a miracle of grace in which man would have no share, but by turning away from the old, which by grace becomes his own merit, and also by living within the unity he is offered. At the beginning of the letter, Paul had sketched this unity as coming entirely from God, consequently, as pure grace proceeding from the Father in the recapitulation of all things in the Son and in the seal of the Holy Spirit. He now shows the execution of this plan in detail, and here man's co-operation, his involvement in this process makes its appearance. Here it is no longer possible to decide what comes from God and what comes from man. When, for example, the thought occurs to a man that he could do something for God's sake, like give alms to a poor man, then this thought stems from God's grace; it would never have occurred to the man without God. But it also stems from the man himself, from whom God let it arise. The same will be true for the execution of the deed. God will not contest that the thought was also the man's and will recompense him accordingly.

4:23. *To be renewed in the spirit of your intelligence.*

They have been instructed in Christ. Because he has undertaken the work of renewal and has likewise placed it in their hands as an integral part of his doctrine, the whole process of renewal bears his stamp. They could not accept faith, arrive by faith at the certainty that they must be renewed, and then make independent plans regarding when and in what way this renewal is to be carried into effect. This renewal is not just a naked requirement of faith; it is also planned and directed by it. For it takes place wholly within the word of the Lord, within what they have heard. It is a renewal *in the spirit of your intelligence*; it comprises, therefore, what they understand, what they occupy their minds with, what they have a judgment about; but all this is carried by a direction found in the spirit. This spirit is in turn unity; and as such it also creates a unity between itself and their spirit, in which once again no demarcation is perceptible. Their spirit is taken into possession by the Holy Spirit, just as their life was previously taken into possession by the eternal life of the Lord. Thus they are now believers, who allow all their thoughts and insights to be renewed in them by the Holy Spirit. In the Spirit they are passive in order to be able to become active. Surrendered, simply letting be, given over, in order to come to a new consistency and activity as selves in the Spirit.

4:24. *And to put on the new man, created according to God in justice and holiness of truth.*

The Lord teaches believers to put on the new man. He does it, not by depicting the new man and sketching a precise picture of his attributes, but by living him in person. He is this new man. And he does not want just to hold up his life as an example of this new man so that men might see the new man in him and come to know God's requirements; he wants to give them this new man together with his entire life, down to his last relations with the Father, so that they can, as it were, appropriate him and live him themselves. In a quite personal way, the Lord places in the hands of every believer the gift of the new man. The acceptance of the gift means, then, that man so surrenders himself to the Lord in his life and in his understanding of faith that he lives precisely that life which the Lord gives him, in other words, that the unity between his faith and the life of the Lord is embodied clearly in his own life.

This new man is *created according to God*, that is, according to the Father. He is in the state of just having been created. He relates back to the newly created Adam as to a possibility granted anew to every believer thanks to the life of the Lord. The possibility, in the Lord, of becoming a stranger to sin, of knowing sin no longer. Of being so liberated by him that relapse into the old sin is made impossible through the attractive force of the new man who lives by the life of the Lord. Of remaining by the Lord's grace in the state proper to the new man of always just having been born.

This new man is created *in justice and holiness of truth*. The truth now appears as the principal concept; it is the receptacle that contains both the justice of God and his holiness. Righteousness and holiness are in the triune God. For this reason, the Son also possesses them in his Incarnation and offers them to men. In surrendering his life to them, he presents them with the grace to accept righteousness and holiness from him so as to live them personally and to spread them farther from ourselves. And all this in the truth, the eternal, immutable truth of God, in which a guiding principle and safeguard of life are given.

4:25. *Therefore, put aside lying, and let every man speak the truth with his neighbor, for we are members of one another.*

To put aside lying is the same as to put aside the old man; enmity against the truth is enmity against God. We must put aside, that is, we must do something of ourselves, so that something may be done in us. To put aside lying, so that we can put on the new man. Putting it aside, we become capable of speaking the truth with our neighbor, of leading a life of truth through the Son who lives in us. For life talks, even before we utter our words. But it will not be enough to appeal to life when it is time to bear witness to the truth; we must rather be able to speak to our neighbor in words about the truth of God. It is by life and word that our neighbor who sees us is to be seized by the truth living in us and, because it is not our truth but the truth of the Son living in us, to be led into the unity of the truth of God.

For we are members of one another. This is the motivation for the absolute urgency of the command of truth. Even as creatures, we men are already parts of the one universe of God, parts that concern one another and that by an essential law of truth itself are made to communicate their truths to one another, to exchange them and to let them form a single truth. The Son, who comes into the world with God's truth, recapitulates the whole truth of the world in himself, in order to bring it back to the Father. The truer we become, the more men live in the truth, the greater is the share in the truth that the Son can bring back into the bosom of the triune truth. In Paul truth never means a purely theoretical correctness. It contains in its very inmost heart a duty to be fruitful and efficacious. Of course, the compass of the theoretically true does not expand when the truth has an effect, and yet more truth comes into being because the truth also lies precisely in this power of what is theoretically correct to generate effects.

4:26. *If you are angry, do not sin. Do not let the sun set on your anger.*

Anger is in itself not a sin. But it can be an incitement to sin, in its outgrowths and in its stubborn persistence. The Apostle thus gives a practical counsel: not to let the sun set on anger. There is a span, not precisely marked off, that anger may last, and its outer limit is fixed. We are thus supposed to be master of our feelings; what is true of anger is necessarily true of other feelings as well. Here Christian self-mastery is differentiated from the Gentile variety. Gentiles want to control their whole teaching and everything they do. Christians want to have doctrine above them, to be led by it, while they want to have mastery and order in themselves. For them there is a hierarchy of mastery.

It is not in vain that Paul appends the warning against anger to the exhortation to speak the truth with one's neighbor. He knows how difficult it is for those who walk in the faith and in the light of understanding to speak with those who do not believe. Here there can often be an occasion for anger. Anger may be close at hand here; it may occasionally even be kindled: it should not go so far that the believer loses control.

4:27. *Give no ground to the devil.*

If we believe aright, our whole space, our whole life belongs to the Lord, and there is per se no longer any room for the devil in us. But since faith manifests itself in a constant striving and exertion, repulsion of the devil likewise requires a permanent battle. If little by little the believer had a feeling that he was safe and that he no longer needed to be mindful, his power to repel would be paralyzed; a sort of hollow cavity would open up between him and his faith, a pervious, undefended position into which the devil could insinuate himself unnoticed. If we were so dominated by our affections that we no longer mastered them, that would again mean that we had lost vigilance and that the devil had gotten a foothold. The life of faith has precisely for Paul the mark of a strain, of a battle. Inwardly it is a positive act: surrender to the

Lord of everything of one's own; but the corresponding outward expression of this is the repelling of everything that is not of the Lord.

4:28. Let him who was a thief steal no longer, rather, let him exert himself to work honestly with his hands, so that he may have something to share with the needy.

Paul continues to provide examples of how we are to put on the new man. This time he shows that it is not enough to refrain from evil, that one must rather without fail do the good as well. He who has stolen must now become a giver of gifts. If he has earned something honestly, he has not really done so for himself but for the needy. Paul is well aware that even among the believers there is a various collection of former sinners. Because they remain men, they will probably have retained certain bad habits from before, at least at the beginning. Faith does not render the battle against evil superfluous; it merely alters it. The Apostle sketches separate phases of this combat, so that everyone may find something in which he can recognize himself.

The present exhortation has the structure of a confession. It is as if the Apostle receives the confession of the thief in order then to show him how he has to conduct himself. He does not simply take away his longing to possess but transforms it and gives it a new goal. By this expedient he makes the man's new life easier. Not everything in it will be so new that one can no longer find one's bearings. The Apostle's action is thus dependent upon the procedure adopted by the Lord, who conveyed the Old Covenant over into the New: everything that was usable and could have lasting value was carried over intact and allowed to remain in existence.

4:29. *Let no evil word proceed from your mouths but, when it is needful, a good word for edification, so that it may bring a blessing to those who hear it.*

In the middle of this verse there is silence. For we must speak only when it is needful. But even if speech is needed, it must never be evil, for there never exists a need for evil speech. But evil is also everything that is empty of content and void in the sense that it fulfills no purpose and consequently does not justify the breaking of silence. Only the good word calls for it, mindful that the Lord is the Word, that in consequence even the word that is granted to us belongs to and returns to him. Hence, when we open our mouths to speak, it is to pronounce the word of the Lord, which conveys *blessing* and grace. This word must serve for *edification*. But even if we speak edifying words, they should conform to necessity, not to our subjective zeal, to the fullness of our heart, to the cleverness of our insights. We must be silent no less when a good word would be superfluous than when a word would be evil. Paul believes that the truth that is alive in us will so enrich our faith that we will become capable of recognizing when a word is justified. Because it comes from the Lord and embodies him, it communicates *blessing*. We must not let this blessing be lost on account of idle chatter. We should take care that this word, which also embodies and must contain the Lord when it leaves our mouth, accomplishes its purpose: to communicate the grace of the Lord.

4:30. *And do not sadden the Holy Spirit of God in whom you were sealed for the day of redemption.*

After the Apostle has set before our eyes the value of the word entrusted to us, and that ultimately means of the Son who has been entrusted to us, who lives in us in his truth, he shows us that we are not without influence on God. The Spirit of God, who in the name of and by the order of the Father brought about the Son's Incarnation on earth, is intimately involved not only with the earthly destiny of the Lord but also with ours as well. If we misuse the word, we show that we do not understand his holiness and his relationship to the Son. By misusing the word, we desecrate in a certain sense the Son and thereby sadden the Holy Spirit. When Paul designates him here as the *Spirit of God*, he does so in order to exhibit the indissoluble relation of the Spirit to the Father and the Son. Hence, in desecrating the Son, we sadden the Holy Spirit and the Father along with him. The Holy Spirit has sealed us; he has espoused our cause and has placed something like a cloak around the habitation of the Word in the soul, a protection, a surety, an attestation that a unity has been created between the soul and the Word, and in the attestation a guarantee of durability and therein a seal that is honored *on the day of redemption*. Until then we remain in the state created by the indwelling of the Son and by the seal of the Spirit, in order afterward to pass over into another state. The Spirit attests in his sealing that he approves the Son's dwelling in us and, consequently, the sacrifice of the Cross, which made this dwelling possible and to which the Spirit was present as a consenting witness. If the Father is going to acknowledge us on the day of redemption as the brothers of his Son, he will do so not only because the Son lives in us but also because he will recognize in us and upon us the sign of his own Spirit. And when we sadden the Holy Spirit, what we are really doing is denying his work, and through this work our denial touches the Son; and it is not as if we had no idea what we were doing, we do it with full awareness.

The *day of redemption* is the day of our appearance before God, the day on which we personally bring back the Son. The Son was entrusted to us as a word, and we must return him to the Father as a word we have employed, in the same way that we ourselves are returned to the Father by the Son. It is a reciprocal restitution. There exists a sort of double alliance: on the one hand, of the Son and the Spirit with us; on the other hand, of the Son with the Father. The two will be compared on the day of redemption, and on that day it ought to be so that the Father in heaven confirms and seals in heaven the redemption, which the Spirit is already preparing now on earth by his activity of sealing. For we are redeemed from everything in us that could be a hindrance to eternal life.

4:31. *Let all bitterness and resentment and anger and uproar and blasphemy and every sort of wickedness be removed from you.*

Paul enumerates a few things that he assumes were present in the community and belonged to the old man. All this has to disappear in the process of renewal. All the feelings and emotions he enumerates have some sort of relation to the words of believers. As long as all this was present, they would all have to submit to the conviction of lying, because it all contradicts the essence of the Lord, who is the Word. And Word as much in his relation to men as to the Father. On the one hand, all these feelings are aimed at and discharged upon one's neighbor and sin against love for him, but, on the other hand, they also become marks of one's own character, insofar as the sinner makes himself the measure of all things and lives always feeling that he has suffered injustice. He thus sins against the Lord present in him, since the Lord lives together with him in the justice of the Father and in the love that constitutes the essence of the triune God. For this reason there is no place for all these things in the law the Lord has brought to men, ultimately because the presence of the Lord in those who believe cannot be reconciled with such things. They must give way. Paul does not say how; but it is obvious from the context: by the Lord's occupying all the available space, evil is simply forced out.

4:32. *Instead, be kind toward one another, tender, ready to pardon one another, just as God has pardoned you in Christ.*

The good qualities Paul now commends are all directed toward one's neighbor and are proved and confirmed in him. The Father lives in the Son these qualities of the community as our example, letting us partake in his own life at the same time. We cannot be good in a kind of solitary completeness. We can be good only when there is another to receive our goodness, to confirm it, and to live from it. For God is good for us in that he pardons us. Only through reciprocal pardon are we brought closer to God's goodness. God has pardoned us all the wickedness that made up the old man. The sign of his pardon was the coming of the Son. Hence, in pardoning, the Father revealed himself; in pardoning, he even manifested his triune relationship. Since we are those who have been pardoned and to whom the revelation of pardon was addressed, we have been taken in this event into the communion of the Father with the Son and can, by pardoning ourselves, diffuse this communion and draw our neighbor into it. Hitherto there has been frequent mention of the unity of truth in faith, of faith in knowledge and love, of the Son in the Father. Now the concept of unity is extended. When the Father attests to his unity with the Son by going so far as to pardon us in the Son, he lets us partake of this unity not only insofar as we have obtained pardon but, which is infinitely more, insofar as we are pardoners who have been allowed immediately to draw others into unity by pardoning. Because pardoning is an action and an event, everything in the communion of pardoners is still coming to be: the qualities of being good, mild, and forgiving. In correspondence to the fact that God's pardon is ever more, our pardon must also be engaged in a developing realization, without knowing limits and closures.

5:1. *Become, then, imitators of God, as beloved children.*

It is as if we were initiated into the life of God by means of this pardon. God grants us his pardon like a kernel of his essence, and when we apprehend it correctly and pardon ourselves as he pardons, we share in an activity that belongs to the innermost heart of God. His action becomes a germ in us, and if we allow it to grow according to his will, we become, by pardoning, imitators of God. But this quality of God does not stand in isolation; it has become especially plain to us only because under this aspect God has revealed himself to us and has helped us turn over a new leaf. Nevertheless, it exists in connection with all the other qualities God wanted to reveal to us. It is from this quality that our understanding spreads out in all directions; we can lay ourselves open to the operation of all God's other qualities, since their core is always grace, and also give imitation a corresponding extension. We imitate in God only that which he has first brought home to us as worthy of imitation and permanently granted to us, in some sense ready for use. Not as something alien, which we do not know what to do with, but always as something that immediately calls for active participation, that obliges us and must unfold itself.

God grants his grace to us as to *beloved children*; his fatherly love takes care that in this bestowal of grace we know ourselves to be children of God. The perennial gift of pardon is given with such living power that we seem to be perennially receiving anew from it love and the grace of sonship. In this grace we need not fear that we will appear presumptuous when we try to imitate God. We know that with his grace and help we are doing in love what corresponds to his demand.

5:2. *And walk in love, as Christ loved you and handed himself over for us as an oblation and a burnt offering to God for a pleasing odor.*

Love itself does not pursue a changing course, not even in us, because it will always be the love of the Lord. But we must walk within this love that remains the same. We must not stand still in it, not deviate from its path, but develop in it, adjust ourselves more and more to it, let our entire vitality and capacity for change as creatures come into play within love.

It is love *as Christ loved you and handed himself over to God*. The divine love in the Son made him, the Incarnate One, a sacrifice, an *oblation* that is offered up and a *burnt offering* that is consumed. This love, which is the love of the Trinity and which accompanied the Son throughout his life on earth, is an active love, an exigent love. It does not allow the one who walks in it to walk without responding. The Son has given as man the entire answer to this love. He has, out of love for us, offered himself entirely to the Father. The Apostle knows that this love will

not cease making its demands on us either. Even if for
the time being we did not know how to respond to this
demand, we would still always know that the Lord understood the full demand of love and that his sacrificial response—which he gave out of love for us—includes our
response as well. We would know, in other words, that in
order to satisfy the demand, we have to make sacrifices.
By means of sacrifice we attain to an understanding of
what is demanded. If we wanted to walk in love without
letting ourselves be truly affected by its exigent demand,
to walk with a certain caution and at a distance, we could
perhaps overlook its exigent character. But because it is
the love of the Lord, it can in no way stand over against
us; it comprises us from the very outset, because the Lord
has made the sacrifice in our name and because for that
reason his gift is not an exterior accident but concerns us
and touches us and takes effect in our inmost heart. And
it does so immediately as sacrificial love. For he gives us
his love with the same qualities it has in him. No one can
say, therefore: I love God, but so long as God does not
specify the sacrifice he requires of me, I do not have to
sacrifice anything.

5:3. *But every fornication and impurity or avarice must not
even be named among you, as befits saints.*

Holy people live by God's holiness. They walk in it, and
all their thoughts are directed by faith. For the power of
God is great enough to be able so to fill up every believer
that he no longer experiences any other longing except
for this very God-given fulfillment and not merely avoids

but no longer even desires to know what is not in keeping with this holiness, what is sinful. He knows that the holiness of God shares God's quality of being ever greater and is capable of taking such hold of the believer as well that he continually strives for it and finds his whole satisfaction in this striving. So the unholy no longer needs to be known or named, for this is fitting for saints.

To the category of the unholy belong fornication, impurity, avarice; everything man does or wishes for himself so long as he does not know God and his neighbor in God, everything he attempts as a solitary castaway in order to satisfy himself. If Paul began just now from God's pardon in order to commend to us the imitation of God, this quality introduced everything that, in God, we have to strive for and to avoid. But it completely excludes every solitariness of the egoistic man both in what concerns the senses and in what concerns the spirit. The pardoner lives in communion and from it and does so ultimately by the grace of the communion of the Father and the Son in the Spirit, thus, of a communion of holiness, from which every impurity must remain far removed.

5:4. No disgraceful conduct, no buffoonery, no frivolous chatter, which has no place, but rather thanksgiving.

If we are allowed to live as saints, then every aspect of our daily lives must also be conformed to this holiness. We must not be in contradiction to ourselves, any more than God in his triune essence exhibits any contradiction whatsoever. We must not permit the old and the new man to live side by side, but in everything we do and say we must take leave of the old. After Paul has opened to us the way of holiness and of communion in holiness, he reminds us again of his previous affirmation that we must let the word live in us as the Word of God. This word must now be thanksgiving. Thanksgiving that we are not obliged to erect by means of our word any chance community among men but, as believers, are permitted to live within God's communion. Just as all our thinking and striving have to be oriented to this holy communion, so do our words. Nothing in them must be in contradiction to the dialogue between the Father and the Son in the Holy Spirit. If the Son is the Word of the Father who wants to live in us, our word has to offer itself as a vessel to the Word that the Son is. All our talking, even when it is addressed to men, has to be of such a nature that the triune God may hear it, may consider it as being ultimately addressed to him through the Son. But everything we will have to say to God has the form of thanksgiving, because it is all an answer to his grace— thanksgiving conjoined to the thanksgiving of the Son before the Father, thanksgiving, too, in the human communion we have received in grace from God in coordination with Christian mission.

5:5. *Know this: every fornicator, whether he be unchaste or avid of gain, that is, an idolater, has no share in the inheritance of the kingdom of Christ and of God.*

Those who believe live within the inheritance of God, because in faith they have become his children. Everything God possesses in his kingdom he possesses together with the Son and the Spirit. They form a unity of possessing and invite those who believe to dwell within this unity as partakers of their possession. Now, as long as believers hold fast to this truth, nothing impure is mixed in. For it is in order to fulfill God's will, in order to be closer to him and to let themselves be directed even more by him that they want to be heirs, and not for the sake of a personal, private advantage. Rather, in order to experience his love more deeply and to be better able to show him their own love. The reception of love makes them for their part richer in love; they make themselves grow rich in God, in order to be able to enrich in their turn God and men.

No *fornicator*, however, can have a part in this law of love. He excludes himself from it. He covets as a desirable good something that does not lie in God and that, when he possesses it, will distance him even more from God, will not only withdraw the inheritance from him, but will not even make it appear worth striving for any longer. This fornicator can be, according to Paul, *unchaste* or *avid of gain*, that is, can let his fornication act either in the body or in the spirit. In both cases he seeks his own, and from the very outset he excises God from what he thinks desirable. He seeks himself as the center of his world, and in this perpetual movement toward himself, he annihilates in himself the movement toward God. Even if the *share in the inheritance of the kingdom of God* were in itself still open and accessible to him, he would not reach it, because he looks and travels in the opposite direction. He lives in the imagination that he, too, is serving and is subject to something. But his ideal is an idol to whom he has set up a monument in the form of unchastity or covetousness and in which he serves only himself. As an *idolater*, he sacrifices truth to untruth; the truth that is God to the untruth that is himself. His service, which in the end is intended for himself, prevents him in every way from being a servant of God.

5:6. *Let no one seduce you with empty words. For on account of such things God's wrath falls upon the sons of disobedience.*

Paul has already forbidden vain talk among his people. But he knows that empty talk will continue to exist in the world in the mouth of unbelievers. This talk will also always keep affecting those who believe. They cannot live without hearing what they would prefer not to hear. But the Apostle would like to neutralize the effect of empty words in them. They are enjoined to see through such words as empty, to recognize by discernment that they do not lead to God but, on the contrary, lead away from him. As soon as they have acquired this knowledge, they must be consistent, must not let themselves be influenced by such words, much less be led astray. Their innermost direction should not change.

The Apostle gives the reason for this: *On account of such things God's wrath falls upon the sons of disobedience.* As long as there are sinners, the wrath of God will be present as a potency. But it will not unload itself on the just, who love him, but *upon the sons of disobedience,* whose whole mode of conduct makes it plain that they take the direction that leads away from God, that above all they do not want to obey him. The obedience that characterizes the Son's attitude toward the Father while on earth is the means the Son gives us in order to furnish God true proofs of our love, of our will to love. It is obedience that will prevent us again and again from doing what God does not want. But if there are any disobedient men who rise up against God and are sons of rebellion, God will pour out his anger over them *on account of such things*: talk that leads astray, but also listening that lets itself be led astray. For if we allow ourselves to be led astray by such talk, we receive the spirit of disobedience in ourselves and belong together with the sons of disobedience to those upon whom God's wrath will unburden itself.

5:7. *So have nothing in common with them!*

Community with them means: to receive their word and to let it work in oneself and to end by talking just as they do. It would be community in vain talk. But the fact that believers are forbidden to enter into the community of the vain does not mean that every community of love with them is discontinued. The commandment of love of neighbor extends even to the vain. But precisely this commandment will prevent believers from receiving anything from the vain that alienates them from their neighbor or from God. It will, on the contrary, suggest to them those words of the Lord that are suited to draw by the grace of God even the vain into the community of love.

5:8. For you were once darkness, but now you are light in the Lord. Walk as children of the light.

They were darkness, because they did not have faith, did not let God work in them, relied on their own resources. Because these ceaselessly circled in themselves, they created no opening, no window toward the light. Now, however, the light of the Lord has broken through this circuit of darkness. But the Lord is light as the fountain of light; he does not keep it for himself but dispenses it freely. So copiously that everyone can walk in it, even more, can become light himself. The light of the Lord has the power to extinguish our darkness, to fill us up so completely that there is no longer anything dark to be discerned in us; and as long as the light streams in, nothing dark will ever return again either. But as soon as we forbade access to the light of the Lord, his fountain would run dry for us. We would once again wall ourselves up in our darkness and would once more live as if there were no light.

Knowing about the light, we can walk *as children of the light*. In the possession of this light we have a surety; we do not have to question the light, undervalue it, hesitate in its radiance; we have the certainty, which proceeds from the light itself, that we are in the light. This certainty is all the greater in that the light does not come from us. To hesitate means: not to believe that God's light is intense enough to overcome our resistances, to change us. It is to believe that to deal adequately with us, a stronger light would be necessary. But because the Lord is every light, he can take away from us every uncertainty along with our darkness. He is the light par excellence, the total light, so that every attempt to measure his luminosity comes to nothing.

5:9. *For the fruit of the light consists in every sort of goodness, righteousness, and truth.*

Paul gives us the possibility here of recognizing the true light by its fruits. These fruits—goodness, righteousness, truth—are all qualities that have their fullness in God. All the fruits of the light will in turn refer back to the light as to their author. The light itself will in its fruit point to light. The Son is light, as the eternal fruit of the light of the Father. He shines in us by implanting in us his divine qualities as fruits. If these fruits of his light ripen in us, they must have his characteristics and refer back to the light of God as their origin. Once more Paul shows the unity of the truth of God spreading out, so to speak, into other qualities: into goodness and righteousness. The unity of truth is so great that it includes these qualities as well. But it is not endangered as unity by the fact that the fruit becomes ours; rather, it passes through us back into itself and carries us as fruitbearers along with it. The reach of God's unity extends ever more powerfully and encompassingly. For in the end everything must become light again. God's light has such intense power that it appears to force something like an increased light out of our earlier darkness. We would perhaps never have been so grateful to God if he had not saved us out of the darkness of ourselves. Insofar as the light enlightens the darkness more and more, it has the capacity to multiply itself.

Goodness, righteousness, and truth are, of course, all three properties of the one God. But goodness appears especially in the Son, righteousness in the Father, truth in the Holy Spirit. God's unity as light is thereby recast in a new way; the attribution of God's properties to the individual persons also serves to shed a more penetrating, more surprising light on the unity of God's essence.

5:10. *Test what is well pleasing to God.*

The light of God in us is also the light of knowledge and judgment in which one can decide and discern. But the gift of discernment is not given to Christians ready-made; they must exercise themselves in it. The Lord alone possesses it of himself. He communicates it to them, but not without constant coordination with his person, with his moment-by-moment discretion and decision. Therefore, they cannot by themselves discern what is good and evil without consulting the Lord but only by continually referring to the Lord to ask what is pleasing to him and what is not. Because the Lord has bequeathed to them the commandment of love as his commandment, in the love that the commandment itself contains they have the touchstone for what is well pleasing to him. Thus, they do not test what is well pleasing to them, they do not make themselves the measure of value, but they ask according to the Lord and judge according to the criterion of the Lord. In this way their decision remains within the decision of the Lord. This is not lack of freedom but the authentic freedom of love. If they are seized by the love of the Lord, they cannot experience any uncertainty in testing, because the love of the Lord does not disclose to them merely the fact that he loves them but, along with this fact, the sense for what love is to him.

5:11. *And have no part in the unfruitful works of darkness, but convict them.*

For the Christian, having part is always within the fruitfulness of love. It is situated at the point where the Christian is so heavily indebted to the love of the Lord that he has no choice but to have a part in his love. Thus, wherever he has to be fruitful, the fruit is within love and its efficacy. But when it is a matter of the *unfruitful works of darkness*, he must be unfruitful. There is, then, a real will to unfruitfulness. For to have a part always also means: to give a part of oneself, to enter into an exchange. To have dealings with the works of darkness, however, would only mean squandering one's fruitfulness on what is unfruitful. Hence the preceding warning to test first. The value sign in me—whether fruitful or unfruitful—depends on the value sign of the thing to which I devote myself: to the Lord or to the works of darkness.

But convict them. This conviction takes place in the act of testing, which is not complete unless one takes a position. In faith it is impossible to distinguish between good and evil without at the same time making a decision away from evil and toward the good. If we follow Paul's advice, we discern and decide in a single act within this testing.

5:12. *What they do in secret is disgraceful even to say.*

What they do in secret they do in darkness, for in the light
there is no possibility of doing anything in secret. Even
though we never entirely comprehend what the Lord does
in the light, we cannot say that he does it in secret. He
does it openly before the Father and before us, and the
fact that much of it remains hidden from us is due only to
our weak understanding. Unfruitful works, on the other
hand, are performed in darkness, and because they are not
touched by the light, it is also impossible for us to pronounce them in the light. But if we were to pronounce
them in the darkness, we would have part in this darkness
of theirs. Now, this does not mean that we should pass
our lives unaware of evil; but we should know it in the
light, without participation in darkness, and here in the
light means: by applying the Lord's test. Precisely because
the Lord knows no sin, his knowledge of evil is absolute,
just as is his rejection of it. It is by essence that which he
rejects and excludes. In order to know evil in its reality,
we must first betake ourselves obediently into the light
of the Lord; to want to know it without the Lord means
already to have betaken ourselves a part of the way into
evil. The Lord rejects evil in himself; we do not reject it
in ourselves, but in the Lord.

5:13. *Everything that is convicted is made manifest by the light,
for everything that is made manifest is light.*

The light, inasmuch as it comes from the Lord, has in it
the power of decision. It brings out clearly the contrasts;

it reveals things to the very last. But this revelation takes place in no light other than the light of the Lord; one cannot separate the two things from each other. The capacity of the light to divide is tied to the Lord's property of deciding. We decide and afterward discern in the light of the Lord. Before it was otherwise; discernment was the first thing, and only after that followed the decision. Now it is more the case that the light makes the decision, and we receive discernment within this decision. We receive it as a result of the property of the light by which it remains entirely in the Lord. When a man makes decisions, they have in a very relative sense the character of his personality. Whether he loves this or that flower, this or that book, will bring out some perhaps superficial trait of his character. But when the Lord makes decisions, not only a single character trait, but his whole person lies in this decision, this "predilection". He reveals in it his whole, immutable nature, while the predilections and opinions of men are infinitely mutable. The Lord's teaching, his foundation, the Church, his Eucharist, are the same today as two thousand years ago and are still just as relevant, while the decisions of the men of that time retain historical value at best. The light of the Lord is therefore decision and thence conviction of all things in him.

For everything that is made manifest is light. Because it has been placed so completely in the light that it receives a fruitful share in the light. Since the light is never indifferent, but decision, it also demands decision from that which is illuminated. In this way the light can also summon to conversion and carry it through. As soon as the evil man recognizes the light as light, he already feels himself drawn into decision. He is enlightened toward knowledge, toward decision. If he allows knowledge and decision into himself, he himself becomes light. He who wants to partake only of knowledge and not of decision does not come to the light. The ultimate illumination is possible only in the unity of discernment and decision as it characterizes the light of the Lord.

5:14. Wherefore it says: Sleeper, awake and arise from the dead, and Christ will enlighten you.

The sleeper is he who does not decide. By waking up he is to render evidence that he is preparing himself to decide. Arising from the dead means the abandonment of all unfruitfulness in order to pass over to the fruitfulness of Christ, not by one's own power, but because Christ illuminates us. Man's contribution consists of awaking and arising; it is the precondition for the Lord to perform the decisive action: draw into the light. He who will not decide cannot be drawn into the decision of the Lord. There is a will to be awake, to be fruitful, which must encounter the greater will of God in order to accomplish all the works of wakefulness. There is this previous act, which still does not know that it is already comprised within God's deed (just as the sleeper does not know that he is waking up), so that the merit may not only be ordered to grace but may be a moment within grace; like crossing the threshold to it, but already drawn by it. The step into the sun, which has already been shining all along.

5:15. *So see to it that you walk carefully, not like fools, but like wise men.*

This is the consequence of the foregoing. The light imposes an obligation. If we know that we are illuminated by the Lord himself, we must not forget this knowledge for one instant in our walk. Our whole daily life proceeds in this light, which illuminates it with the ultimate, absolute clarity and objectivity of God, which at the same time is his decision. The attention, circumspection, and conscientious care of our walk should correspond to the majesty of this light. In it we must not behave like fools by fancying, for example, that we could determine and choose our actions ourselves and calculate their bearing outside of the light, but as *wise* men, that is, as men who are aware, who always bear in mind that the light decides and that a decision made outside the light would be distinguished and divided from the light. This care, then, has to orient itself to remaining in the light and to the knowledge that the light never becomes a function of ourselves but always remains the light of the Lord.

5:16. *Buy up the time, for the days are evil.*

The works of the Christian also have a relation to time. He must know, in other words, what time is, what it is worth, and he must know how to proportion his works to the price of time. Every time stands in a relation to eternity, and although full value belongs to eternity alone, God has nonetheless meted out from this eternity a determinate value to every instant. The Christian must order his works according to the preciousness of the instant; he must enter into a sort of contest with time; he must ascribe to his actions as much weight as the time has; in spite of that, he will always fall short of the time's value.

For the days are evil. They run to nothing without men's having given them this fullness willed by God. The Son entered into time and brought men his entire message, whose aim is to reengage them in service. But they have not accepted this reengagement. They do not want to place time in the service of eternity; they prefer to leave time its seemingly natural course, without a link to God. They consider time a function of their own existence. For this reason the days are evil, because they use them according to their sinful purposes. They not only alienate themselves from the Son and his message but, by so doing, likewise alienate themselves from the Father and from his gift of time, which as his gift ought always to serve his eternal and holy ends. But because the days are evil, evilly filled up and evilly used, Christians have the obligation to redeem the time. They are from the very outset directed to this work of supererogation, which consists of buying back not only their own time but also time in general, the time of those who squander it, or better: buying it up with something of value: with their sacrifice, with their word, with their obedience, all things that have their worth in God alone, just as time in the final analysis has its value only in God. There is a hint of the idea of expiation in this demand of Paul. Individuals must act this way as members of the Church, which as a whole is summoned to supererogation, in the sense that everything God gives her should always reflect back into his being ever more and ever greater.

5:17. *Therefore, do not be injudicious but full of understanding, which is the will of the Lord.*

Time, this good gift of God, has become a wicked, evil time on account of men's sin. If, then, even God's gifts can be so corrupted by men, the admonition of the Apostle not to be *injudicious* is doubly justified. But in order not to trigger this effect, which reveals the might of the power of sin, they must have insight into the will of God. This insight holds the secret of maintaining God's gifts pure. This insight is not only an outward expression of their understanding but a submission of the whole man. The actual existence of this insight is proved only when the whole man demonstrates by his whole bearing that he has also personally assimilated what he has understood. He cannot demonstrate the reality of his insight except by doing the will of the Lord, the will he has just understood. Insight operates in him like a catalyst, by immediately placing his powers into a new bond that transforms the mental act of understanding into the all-encompassing act of obedience to God.

Paul resumes the foregoing with the word *therefore*. If the days had not become evil, if sin had not won the upper hand, men would have had no need whatsoever to understand God's will in this intellectual manner. They would have remained in God's will with a sort of naïveté; indeed, they would not have needed to distinguish God's will from their own at all. Only because of the fall did the will of God sift itself out as something separate from man's will, which had become disobedient. Previously, man had lived in the will of God. Without grasping it intellectually, but rather comprehended and understood within its grasp.

5:18. *And do not intoxicate yourselves with wine, in which there is intemperance, but have your fullness in the Holy Spirit.*

Paul knows—both from his own past and by general knowledge of man—that man strives without quarter after a fullness. He needs something to fill him up, to complete him, to permit him to realize his uttermost possibilities. If this fulfilling reality does not penetrate into him, he will always suffer want. Now, however, he feels his own emptiness; it perpetually makes him aware of his limits; it paralyzes his boldest undertakings. If he makes plans, he must reckon with the little he possesses; and even if he were to exploit to the full the capital of his life, in the end he would still inevitably run up against the barriers of incapacity, against the ultimate boundary of his power, against the impossibility of realizing his dreams. He therefore searches for means of forgetting and transcending these barriers. If he seeks them in the intoxication of wine, then he falls into *intemperance*. He has removed a certain limit, but only to run up against another one that is far narrower. He lives a life of illusion. Not only in the risk but in the certainty of going astray at any moment. The realization of his longing withdraws even farther than if he had kept to his natural limits. Intemperance renders impossible not only the execution of one's plans but also the plan itself, which is internally fragmented and distorted.

But have your fullness in the Holy Spirit. The Holy Spirit is that miraculous means that the Creator has made available to every one of his creatures in order to round out its lacks and insufficiencies. This fulfillment is not realized within the narrow limits of the creature but leads into the fullness of God. It is left to the Spirit to take charge of erasing the creature's limits, of fixing other, new limits, finally, of taking over human plans in order to direct their continued course into his plans, which are limitless. To be filled up by the Spirit always means to renounce whatever is mine and I have a total picture of and to be carried over by the Holy Spirit into obedience to the triune God, Father, Son, and Spirit.

5:19. *Speak to one another in psalms and hymns and spiritual canticles, singing and rejoicing in your hearts.*

If Paul expresses the wish that we might live in the fullness of the Spirit, so that he rules in a living way our whole life, he knows that this will not succeed without our cooperation. We must make a personal effort to converse with one another in the language of the Spirit. It is not our petty cares and concerns, our needs, hopes, and apprehensions, or even the good we do or desire, that is to be our topic of conversation, but exactly what is suggested to us by the Spirit and has him as its content, such as every form of spiritual canticle. It is from this source that we are to draw our thoughts and mental occupations, so that what we communicate to others may be, not of us, but of God. The words we use to converse with God must also give their characteristic stamp to the words we use in our Christian conversation with one another. In this way both we ourselves as well as our interlocutors are placed in an atmosphere of God.

But Paul says: *Speak with one another.* It is those who are already believers who can speak with one another in this way. Outsiders would not understand these words before being initiated into the faith. But if psalms and hymns give their imprint to our everyday speech, the words we have at our disposal to explain ourselves to them become ever more lively and appropriate. Not, as it were, by imposing from above a sort of foreign vocabulary on our everyday speech, but by impressing on our entire daily life the sense of the psalms and hymns and thus accustoming our quotidian reality to the supernatural world in virtue of the word of God that is contained in these spiritual canticles. Our human intercourse is thereby blown wide open, as it were, for God himself is drawn into it; the singing and jubilation that are due to the Lord do not come to a halt on account of our everyday conversation. The Lord is not only the content of our conversation through his Word but, in view of the praise owing to him, is also its end. We bring one another closer to God by means of our conversation.

5:20. *Say thanks always for everything in the name of our Lord Jesus Christ to God the Father.*

Thanksgiving presupposes that one knows what one has to give thanks for. This knowledge comes from the

Spirit, in whom we are enjoined to have our fullness. We are told to give thanks for everything, because the Spirit places us in a position to understand everything as a motive for thanks. Thanks are directed to God the Father, but in the name of the Son. The Spirit thus brings us to the point where we not only accept thankfully everything we receive personally but also give thanks in the name of the Son for that for which the Son gives thanks to the Father. We enter into a closer communion with the Son, a communion that finds its foundation and basis in thanks. It is through his thanks to the Father that the Son establishes this communion, in that he simply draws us into it as believers. Our thanks must be rendered *always*. In other words, our first business is not to subject God's gifts to examination in order to decide which ones we want to give thanks for and which ones not, but to pay our thanks prior to every test and every understanding of the content of these gifts. It is in this way that the Son gave thanks, and the Apostle associates us here completely to the incarnate Lord, who came to teach men the right attitude of thanks toward the Father. The Father who as author of all things, and above all as Father of the ever-thanking Son, has a claim to our perennial thanks.

THE DUTIES OF THE STATES IN LIFE

5:21. *Subordinating yourselves to one another in the fear of Christ.*

Within the thanks they have to present to the Father in the name of the Lord, Christians are to be subordinate to one another; thanksgiving and subordination are meant in the Lord's teaching to form a unity. The subordination demanded is in this context not yet subordination to the ecclesiastical hierarchy but, in a very general sense, a reciprocal subordination of all believers. Every believer has regard for the other, but this regard does not rest primarily upon personal esteem but depends chiefly upon the *fear of Christ* and also flows out of the attitude of thanks. By the Lord's command, every believer has the duty to love his neighbor. But this love imposes upon him a duty of submission toward his fellow believer, who has assumed the responsibility of love for the Church. Paul describes this submission simply by giving it the name of fear. Christian fear, which has its origin in love of the Lord and brings out clearly the distance between the Lord and us. The fruit of this fear is submission. Insofar as the faith, thanks, and the fear of Christ are all conditioning causes of this submission, they will all leave their mark on it. It will not be a submission dependent upon human motives and tinged with sin, which continually threatens to run off the rails, but a subordination that elevates man and connects him more closely to the Lord. A subordination that allows one to consider the word of another as more important than one's own because the word of the Lord is reflected and acknowledged in it. This general reciprocal subordination already stands therefore quite close to the ecclesiastical-hierarchical order, as will emerge in the next verse. It is noteworthy that Paul shows how this fear develops in its entirety out of the foregoing: love and thanks. Outside the context of this connection, these new requirements would not be understood rightly.

5:22. *You women, be subject to your husbands as to the Lord.*

Hitherto Paul has not distinguished between man and woman in his general portrayal of the Christian's attitude. He was addressing all alike, and his words were applicable to all without distinction. He now turns to the individual sexes and starts by delineating the task of the woman: she is to be subject to her husband. This is nothing new, because it has already been demanded of everyone that they subordinate themselves to one another. Even this subordination was nothing new, because all of them had already been practicing it toward the Lord. The attitude of the woman is thus deduced from the attitude of every Christian in relation to the Lord; and it goes without saying that every Christian is subject to the Lord and lives by the Lord's obedience toward the Father in order to obey him, the Lord. Yet in the case of the woman, this subjection is formulated in a particular manner: she is to be subject to her husband *as to the Lord.* This does not mean being obedient in two separate relationships and acts, on one side to the Lord and on the other to her husband, but—this is what is meant by the word *as*—to both in a unity of obedience. Hence, obedience characterizes the whole existential attitude of the woman; if she has a husband, she has to practice it toward her husband as if to the Lord; if she has no husband, toward the Lord. Her relationship to the Lord is not infringed upon by her married state insofar as marriage appears as a sort of extension to her husband of her obedience vis-à-vis the Lord, a sort of practical, visible application of her relationship to the Lord. If Paul previously developed the collective attitude of the community from the love of the Lord, he now explicates the particular attitude of the woman in terms of her position relative to the Lord, which, however, the Lord himself lives as exemplar and source in his relationship to the Father.

5:23. *For the man is the head of the woman, just as Christ is the head of the Church, he, the redeemer of his body.*

In her role of obedience, the woman is now likened to the Church: she is the body, the man is the head. As the body, she has to follow the judgment of the head, and the archetype of this relationship is presented to her in the order that obtains between Christ and the Church. It is the role of Christ the head to lead and to decide. If the man is allotted by the Lord the task of imitating him as head, then he will have to keep strictly to the original, Christ. If he does, if he carries out his role as head according to the mind of Christ, then the life of the woman,

if she is married, is charted and steered by his leadership
and planning. She is given a line to which she can read-
ily accommodate herself. If the man patterns himself on
Christ and receives his instructions from him, he cannot
arbitrarily use and misuse the subjection of the woman
for his human ends; he must form her with her help in the
same way that the Lord uses the subjection of the Church
to form her. For this reason, the woman will constantly
have the Church before her eyes as a prototype insofar
as she is the body; she will again and again find a norma-
tive mirror of herself in the various manifestations of the
Church's life, not, however, as if this mirroring went no
farther than herself and the Church, but in the sense that
every aspect of her relationship to the Lord is unveiled in
its proper dimensions. Just as she must seek contact with
the Lord in the Church, in order to understand the prototype, in the same way her marital obedience means that
she must always perceive the Lord behind her husband.
The Lord, who guides her husband, whom her husband
obeys, gives her not only himself as head, he gives her
the man as a kind of illustration of his grace of headship.
The man reveals to her the Lord; in him and behind him
she sees the Lord, though this does not imply that the
man's part is diminished, for to the degree that he obeys
the law of the Lord, he can and must demand the subjection and compliancy of the woman. Because the Lord is
the perfectly obedient one and perfectly living one, and
perpetually gives his Church these characteristics that are
properly his own, the Church, strengthened by the love
of the Lord, ought to be perpetually obedient and alive,
and every marriage endowed with the characteristics of

the Lord and the Church ought in the relation of obedience to include their undiminished vitality and never be at the end of its possibilities.

5:24. But as the Church is subject to Christ, so too let wives be subject to their husbands in all matters.

The Lord, as the Son whose generation from the Father is forever always just now happening, lives in a submission to the Father's loving will that is eternally just now taking place. If the Church wishes to be the genuine bride of the Lord, then she must forever remain in that instant when she is generated by the will of the Lord. In the attitude of subjection proper to one who is just now obtaining something by the favor of another. At the moment of her generation she obtains simultaneously her being in the absolute and her fullness. If she ever lost the characteristic of being generated of God, her subjection to the Lord would be in extreme peril. She must remain through all ages in the moment of her springing up from the Lord in order to maintain through all ages her subjection, in order to receive and to accomplish the will of the Lord that is always just now made known to her. The same holds for the woman, whose actual passage from virgin to bride is, after all, due to the choice and courtship of the man. At the moment of wooing, when she acquires the new property of being a bride, she feels herself quite willing to be subject to the man, in order to receive bridehood in its full purity. She binds herself without conditions to the man who has chosen her, who loves her. Because this moment—which has its archetype in the moment when the Bride-Church springs into existence —is something so fundamental in the life of the woman, the requirement that she be subject flows out of it as an entirely obvious consequence. She should always remain the same woman upon whom her suitor bestowed his attentions and who received the gift of bridehood from him. She should not consider the courtship as a moment belonging to the past, which immediately yields to other, more important things, but should make that moment an abiding form of her existence. The subjection, which in the first act of saying Yes appears to be the most obvious thing in the world, should also remain so in the times that follow, since it must become deed and life. If the reciprocal relationship of the origin—the wooing of the man and the willingness of the woman—remains the foundation of their marriage, they are as close as possible to the archetype of the Lord and the Church that is continually coming into being out of him. It behooves the woman to become and to be the woman whom the man chose, not the one whom she decided upon. For she gave her word of consent to the choice of the man. The man, however, cannot shape the life of the woman capriciously; inasmuch as he has Christ as head, he is likewise bound. What Paul outlines here is the framework of Christian marriage. He does not touch upon pagan marriage. He is writing to Christians and is presenting Christian life to them according to the norms of Christianity.

5:25. You husbands, love your wives, just as Christ himself loved the Church and handed himself over for her.

Paul now addresses himself to men, not as to a separated parcel of the community, but as to the complement, in order to bring out once again the unity for which he is always mindful. When he spoke to women, there was already mention of the role of the man, and in the same way there is now also mention of the role of the woman. Both have to be better initiated into their common task of Christian unity in marriage.

Love your wives. This is an imperative that brooks no qualification. What follows merely gives it its orientation and justification: *just as Christ himself loved the Church.* That is, with the love that is the love of the Lord, an applied love of the Lord that he bestows upon his Church and is known to the community. Whoever lives in the Church, which is to say, by faith, lives by the love of the Lord, which accompanies him everywhere. He is surrounded by it on all sides, he has received innumerable proofs of its presence. It is out of this love experienced by all that men are to shape their relationship to their wives. Since the reciprocal love of man and woman stems from the love of the Lord, every marital love must lead back to the Lord and strengthen both the man's and the woman's love for the Lord.

Paul throws into relief a particular trait of the love of the Lord, in order to hold it up to men for imitation: the Lord *handed himself over* for his Church in love. In his love he no longer distinguished between the Church and himself; he handed himself over for her to such a degree

that in this act it is no longer possible to state how much
the Lord gives and how much of what the Church has
received she gives back in her answer. Men must love in
a like handing over of themselves. They must, as it were,
apprehend the moment when the Lord consummates the
act of handing himself over, a moment that appeared in
time but was an expression of a whole eternity and, therefore, will not be surpassed even in the whole course of
time, either in the Lord or in the man who hands himself
over for his wife. His handing himself over must have
the force of an act, of a moment in which the uttermost
self-giving is accomplished and yet must display the to-
kens of durability. As if every abatement and weakening
in love were unworthy of a Christian.

5:26. *To sanctify her, purifying her by the bath of regeneration
in the word.*

In order to be able to love his Church, the Lord purifies her and does so ceaselessly. If she did not always receive purity from the Lord, the Church would not possess
it. She receives it in baptism. Indeed, she really receives
it by becoming a copartaker of the purification granted
to one of her children at every new baptism. After the
Lord has purified her, he sanctifies her. Two phases of the
same event are distinguished here: purification must lead
the way in order to open the possibility of sanctification.
It may be said that the Lord does to his whole Church
what the Church undertakes in regard to her single members when, for example, she purifies them by confession
and, within this purification, also makes them partakers

of sanctification. Men are instructed to comport themselves as did Christ. It is as if they were burdened with the responsibility for their wives' becoming holy. But this is possible only if a kind of integration between the role of the man and that of the Lord takes place, that is, if men allow him to take them entirely to himself and, permanently handed over to him, imitate what he does. Not only outwardly, but by having the same attitude toward him as he has toward the Father, and then out of this free obedience to treat their wives just as the Lord treats his Church. Just as the relationship of the Lord to the Church never closes in upon itself but immediately leads back to the Father—which means that the purification and sanctification of the Church issue in the glorification of the Father—so, too, men are answerable in their relation with their wives, in the sense that they have to lead them purified and sanctified back to the Son.

In the Word. The word is the expression of the Lord; he speaks it, and he is it. He communicates himself in every word he says. The word he pronounces is not detached from him; it is not a doubling of his being; on the contrary, it is one with him. The word is the sign of his most intimate self-giving to the Church, since he gives himself in the word and places this word in her. Thus the word of the man to the woman should also remain in the Lord an expression of his love that hands itself over and, beyond that, an expression of the Lord's handing over his life to his Church for the glorification of the Father.

5:27. In order to form for himself a glorious Church, having neither spot nor wrinkle nor anything of the sort, but in order that she may be holy and blameless.

The Lord forms for himself his Church, and the formation is constant. This means that the Church is not her own end; she has her end in the Lord. Her existence fulfills a wish of the Lord. He requires her, not for others, but *for himself*. By forming her, he shows that he really does have need of her, for he does nothing without a reason, nor does he do anything to which one can ascribe a meaning only after the accomplished fact. Because he has to rely on her in this way, he forms her from the very outset precisely as he needs her to be; she must have *neither spot nor wrinkle nor anything of the sort*. He makes her worthy of him and does not tolerate the presence in her of anything that is not *holy and blameless*. She is to be like him. In order to achieve this, he must ceaselessly be in the process of building and forming his Church. If she were left to herself for a moment, she would immediately forget that her end is in him and would let men give her such a different form that she would be estranged from the Lord and he would no longer be able to recognize his holiness in her.

He makes her *glorious* and full of majesty. She partakes of the glory he came to reveal. Her formation is a part of his glorification of the Father. Here it is manifest that even what he prepares for himself serves the fulfillment of the Father's will. The Church is thereby set from the very beginning at the place of his own obedience vis-à-vis the Father. She can never consider herself an indepen-

dent construction, which might have been made at some
time or other by the Lord and afterward left to herself.
She must rather have a disposition analogous to every
word the Lord spoke on earth; she is a portion of his
fulfillment of the Father's will and must remain exactly
at this spot, in order to be able to draw her life from the
holiness of the Lord. If she displayed spots, she would
thereby demonstrate her estrangement from the Lord or
act as if she supposed her own unholiness also existed in
the Lord. She would be in the process of apostatizing.
Inasmuch as she is a Church willed and formed by the
Lord, however, she cannot do otherwise than turn her
whole countenance, pure and holy, to her bridegroom.

*5:28. Therefore, husbands must love their wives as their own
bodies. He who loves his wife loves himself.*

As the Lord, being the head, loves his Church as his body,
so too husbands must love their wives. As the Lord ceaselessly purifies his body, so too husbands must purify their
wives, so that they can love them as the Lord loves his
Church. As the Lord is perennially in the process of pro-
ducing for himself his Church, in order to give her to
the Father for his glorification, so too must the husband
perennially produce his wife. He must preserve her just
as he formed her as a bride for himself when he courted
her, and the woman must remain for her husband in the
state of becoming a bride, just as the Church does for
her Lord. Husbands have to love their wives *as their own
bodies.* They love their body because God has bestowed it
upon them as a gift, so that by its means they may carry

out his intention. They do not love it chiefly because it belongs to them but because it makes possible their service of God. Because God created every man as body and soul at once and the body can be an expression of the soul. When the man takes a wife, then this wife has to be drawn into the same love, which is intimate love of the service of God. Since the woman is one flesh with the man, she must become one with the love the man has for his body.

He who loves his wife loves himself. The Lord has decreed love of neighbor as his commandment: Love thy neighbor as thyself. He does not command love of self, he presupposes it. But he does not mean thereby a selfish disposition that would be circumscribed by man himself and would find its goal in him, but a love of gratitude toward the Creator. We have to love ourselves, because God has loved us first and because to serve and glorify him we have to love everything he loves. We love ourselves as belonging to him, with his love, which comes from him and goes back to him and stops in us along the way only insofar as it thereby furthers us in our service. If we did not love ourselves at all, then we would be in contradiction to God, who loves us. By loving us, he imposes upon us the duty of likewise loving ourselves, but in the same spirit. We stand before God as a sort of mirror, and we perceive his love, which is reflected in us, but only in order to send it back to him immediately. It is in this way that the man must love the woman: within a love that, coming from God, goes back to God and beholds in the woman, as in his own body, the gift of God's love.

5:29. *For no one has ever hated his own flesh, but nurtures it and cherishes it as Christ does the Church.*

Christ produces the Church for himself, while we possess a body that God the Father has produced for us. Although we are not the producer of our body, there is nevertheless a similarity between the two bodies, in that both are enlisted from the very outset in service: the body in our service, the Church in the service of the Lord. Since we need it for our service, since it is drawn into our commission, which has its ultimate origin in the sending of the Son, whose purpose is to glorify the Father, we too love our body and take care of it. The service the body performs for us is something, not external or secondary, but indispensable. Hence, our care for it has a certain similarity to the care the Lord has bestowed upon the Church and is therefore included in love for the Church. This inclusion is decisive for Christians; their love for the body is in order when it has its place completely within the Lord's love for the Church. What we are obliged to do for our bodies has its measure in the final end of the body: its enlistment in service. Otherwise, we could easily arrive at the very border of sin. We should be too severe with our body rather than too soft, because the Lord too must constantly be strict with the Church, in order to preserve her always in the state of coming into being and not to let her degenerate into being an end to herself in any way.

5:30. *For we are members of his body.*

The Lord, who in his love embraces the Father as well
as men, who was generated by the Father in order to be
God together with him, let himself be sent by the Father
and accepted a body like we have in order to be man
together with us and in this way to bring us back to the
Father. By giving us his Eucharist at the moment of his
return to heaven, he granted us a perpetual share in the
mysteries of his life, so that by sharing in his flesh we
could be called members of his body in an equally real,
fleshly sense. But he gave his Eucharist to the Church, to
his bride-body, which he formed for himself on earth and
which he created, so to say, without members, to give
us the chance to incorporate ourselves into him and to
become his members. It is through us that the Church is
to remain living and to receive ever-new life. The more
mysteries we learn from the Lord, the more firmly and
forcibly are we drawn into the divine mystery of our being members of his body. The Lord wants to continue
to exercise functions in his members, indeed, to awaken
in his body new functions necessary to it as a whole by
dispensing new mysteries. Some mysteries of his body
appear fully comprehensible to us only when they are
distributed among the members of his body, the Church,
and lived in conformity with him. No one can withdraw
and say that the body already has enough members. The
body is complete only when all the members really want
to function, and not according to a gradation of rank, as
if only the most important organs were responsible for
sustaining the body, while the others could afford to pull

back as being inessential, but in that all, showing the same commitment, want to pledge themselves for the life of the body. They cannot, however, do it by themselves but only by the grace given them by the Lord of being allowed to be a member and to render the very service he demands. He himself demands it, not by his own authority, but by the great demand of the Father, which he made an integral component of the Lord's mission. So that in the end, the members' service to the body is fully realized in the Lord's own service of glorifying the Father, which he alone is capable of performing but which he invites us to carry out along with him, as if we were equally necessary and equally entitled to do so.

5:31. *Therefore man will leave father and mother and cling to his wife, and the two shall become one flesh.*

The man cannot be definitively bound in two directions. If he believes, he has the great bond to God, and this can be represented within the bounds of earthly life by one human bond alone. Since man and woman are created for each other, he will leave the first bond of the family to cling to his wife. That they *become one flesh* is wholly included in the new bond. It is not something preliminary, subject to free disposition, but something so definitive that it is included in the definitiveness of this clinging. A sort of process thus occurs: leaving, clinging, being one flesh. This being one flesh is not something transitory. It is abiding. Even during the period when the woman bears to term the fruit of the man, the man's body is one flesh with the woman. Dissolution is no longer possible, because this unity is rooted in the spirit, in the bond created by clinging, a bond that clasps them so firmly they can no longer remove themselves from it.

It is the man who must cling to the woman, not the woman to the man. The woman is naturally subject, so this clinging is not her affair. The man has to cling in his courtship; he has to show the unbreachable strength of the bond. When the man has said to the woman: I bind myself to you, then the possibility of being subject is opened up for the woman. She cannot be subject before the bond is fastened by the man. The man must bind himself even before the woman binds herself. He thereby spares the woman the humiliation of submitting herself spontaneously on her own initiative. He has to take the risk first, since he does not yet know whether the woman will accept his courtship. That is his humiliation, while the humility of the woman will consist in the submission that follows.

5:32. *This mystery is great, but I say it in reference to Christ and the Church.*

The Apostle puts the mystery of the binding of man and woman back into the much greater context of the relationship between the Lord and his Church. He has presented the man-woman relationship at such length only so that the relationship of the Lord and the Church might appear more vividly. Between men there are perhaps no livelier and more easily expressible relations than those between man and woman, but for Paul the Christ-Church relationship is even more essential and more vital. Everything said about marriage ought to exist on a much greater scale where the Lord and the Church are one. Christ is one flesh with his Church. This is perhaps the greatest mystery in Christianity, and the Lord was always at work on it through all the years of his activity, through his whole Passion and his return to heaven. What is more, the mystery of the redemption was *one* mystery within this mystery and was ordered to it. Every word the Lord says inside the Church, because the two are one flesh, can be apprehended and explained in a most intimate sense. Where the Church is one flesh, she possesses the Spirit as well, in order to convey everything the Lord says and in such a way that it becomes a living, obliging truth in every single member. Outside of the Church the words of the Lord are robbed of the vitality of their truth; they exist in isolation here and there, as if torn from the root of their life. If the Father is perennially in the act of generating the Son, the Lord is perennially generating his Church. He generates her in a sort of dependence upon the Father's generation. He generates her by receiving her wholly into himself, by perennially impressing upon her the characteristics of his divinity, and by seeking to draw her into the triune truth that can be perceived nowhere more vitally than in his bride. Though he reveals to her his mysteries, they are always at the same time the mysteries of the Father and the Holy Spirit. Even though at the time of his Incarnation they received a human guise, which makes them comprehensible, these mysteries have not ceased to be divine and to belong to the Trinity. Whenever the Son gives away something of his life, he always discloses at the same time the life of the Father and

of the Spirit. If he is one with his Church to the point
that he forms one flesh with her, he effects this mystery
within the mystery of his being one with the Father and
the Holy Spirit.

5:33. *Accordingly, let each one of you love his wife as himself,
but let the woman fear her husband.*

Paul concludes his teaching about marriage with a recapitulation of what has been said. A certain priority of the
man has been clearly established; he possesses the love,
the woman is to have the reverence. This simple reality
is infinitely enlarged by the fact that through the marital
relationship, Paul is aiming at the ecclesial relationship.
That the Lord loves his Church is clear, and the men are
to pattern themselves on this reality. The Church (and
the men belong to the Church as well), however, must
have an enduring reverence toward the Lord: in everything that she does, that she lets be done to her, that she
decides and arranges, she is to remain within the attitude
of reverence. This reverence has to be her answer to the
love of the Lord, her form of love by which she can most
properly answer the infinite love of the divine Son. The
love with which he loves her is the same as that with
which he loves the Father. He does not have two qualities of love; his whole love is divine; and before this love,
what can the Church do but stand in the greatest reverence? Perhaps this is the hardest thing demanded of the
Church: that she never pass to a sort of equal status. That
she persevere to the very end in the attitude of subjection. That to the very end she hear what the Lord has to

say to her, leaving to him the form of speech, submitting to him as well the consequences of his love. In the same way, the woman leaves to the man the shaping of love, always awaiting everything from his love, never anticipating anything. This reverential fear of the woman before the man is not a quality in its own right but, among Christians, derives from the Church's reverential fear before the Lord. Thus, the entire relationship is ultimately shaped by the living love of the Lord; it is this love that awakens and brings forth the readiness, the reverential fear, the whole answer of the Church.

6:1. *You children, obey your parents in the Lord, for this is just.*

After Paul has spoken of the Christian relationship between man and woman, he proceeds to the relationship of children and parents. It is once again the Lord who gives the entire relationship its form. In principle, children should obey their parents simply because this is what human order requires. Parents have judgment and can direct the inexperience of children. Yet it is not to this natural order that Paul appeals in order to justify the obedience of children but to the Lord. Christ was obedient to his parents; his obedience to them was a part and an application of his obedience to the Father, and his parents were likewise obedient; they had placed themselves entirely at the disposition of God's will so that the Son could fulfill his mission. Both the child and the parents were comprised within the will of the Father, so that it was impossible for any conflict to arise between them. Paul places this archetypical pattern before his people when he says *in the Lord.* Because the Lord lived his obedience so simply and so manifestly at Nazareth and during his whole life up to his Passion and death, it should not be difficult for children and parents to imitate him. *For this is just.* The obedience of the Son has its origin in the justice of the Father and is performed in love; strictly speaking, we see love in him more than justice. But the two are indissolubly interwoven, just as the New Covenant cannot be separated from the Old. The Son himself is the perfect unity of obedience and love, and this corresponds to the justice of the Father. There reigns everywhere here a perfect absence of conflict, which can be taken in any situation as the criterion of the relationship between parents and children.

6:2. *"Honor thy father and thy mother", this is the first commandment with a promise.*

Paul takes over the old commandment in his teaching on the Christian family, which is developed with constant reference to the obedience of the Lord and his relationship to the Church. The reverence of children for their parents also belongs in this context. The Lord proved his love to the Father by placing at his disposition his entire life and his entire mission with the aim of glorifying him in all things. He has bestowed his relationship to the Father upon the Church, in that he allows her to stand in the same reverence toward him as he does toward the Father. Within the Church children are for their part to live by his reverence by honoring father and mother. Here it is made clear how the old Mosaic commandments retain their *raison d'être* in the New Covenant and live on in a new, deepened form. The Lord has not only kept them but perfectly embodies them, so that now whoever wants to keep the commandment need only look to him.

This is the first commandment with a promise. In the Old Covenant, then, the commandment had not been given as something already concluded; it led farther. It contained a promise that a father wishes for his children and every man wishes for himself. The commandment of God is like a conversation, almost like an agreement: God says what is to be done so that he may have a reason to give his gifts. By this commandment with a promise, man is brought into the fullness of the ecclesial relationship, since in the Church, every word of the Lord, every demand of the Father, is from the very outset tied to a promise. Everything the Church is required to do is taken up into the glorification of the Father and consequently can give to every individual something of the Son's love for the Father and of his mission. Every commandment in the Church is the first step toward something greater, something more full of promise; it is an approach to the Father through the Son.

6:3. *"So that it may go well with you and you may live long upon the earth."*

The promise of the ancient commandment deals principally with natural things, the natural relationship to physical parents, the honor that is their natural due, so that one may attain the sort of happiness that nature desires: a long life upon earth attended by prosperity. That which can fulfill an earthly man. The very fact that he honors his parents will be the beginning of happiness for the natural man, and everything that develops out of it, whether it has an obvious connection or not, will be in continuity with this happiness. But this earthly happiness is part of a promise. If such a promise comes from God, then it cannot be fulfilled outside of the fulfilled promise. Everything, even the resulting happiness, depends upon the character of the promise; it is happiness only because God has promised this connection; and because the promise of the Father most properly speaking is the Son, the happiness that was promised in the commandment will not be bestowed outside of the Son.

6:4. *And you fathers, do not provoke your children, but bring them up with discipline and correction in the Lord.*

Fathers are granted an authority over their children that already has a natural foundation in the advantage of being the adult party and of being in the position of having generated them. The children, who find themselves in an inferior station, can easily feel themselves restricted by this authority, to which they are not equal, and can easily become embittered or dispirited. Particularly when they feel only the authority in it and not the love as well. Paul desires that fathers not misuse their authority and that children increasingly learn to understand paternal authority in a Christian manner. To behold the Father who commands in the Son who obeys. But as the Son partakes of everything that is the Father's, Christian fathers must likewise let their children partake of their love from the very beginning and must educate them by discipline and correction for their adult life. They should not see this as an ultimate reality but as a mediation between the child and God. Through his education, which leads straight to God, the child must learn to understand that even the life of fathers stands in an obedience to God, and they must grow together with their fathers into the Lord's loving obedience to the Father. As the Lord has formed his Church for himself, in order to take her with him to the Father, so too will fathers attempt to form their children according to the mind of the Church, in order to foster their growing up to the Lord in the Church.

6:5. *You slaves, render obedience to your masters according to the flesh with fear and trembling in the simplicity of your heart as to Christ.*

The slaves have lords over them who can command the flesh. Paul had spoken of the flesh a propos of marriage; it was the gift of the man to the woman, of the woman to the man, the possibility of expressing their marital love. Now a new role of the flesh appears on the scene: it can also be for performing services for an earthly lord who is not Christ yet has the right to dispose of it. The slave places his body and the fruit of his labor at the disposition of this master. Paul speaks only of the flesh, not of the spirit. In the flesh the slaves have to acknowledge their distance from their lord and therefore must carry out their work *with fear and trembling*; not with the self-satisfaction and superiority of one who is capable and who, because he works, feels he is on an equal footing with his master or even looks down upon him, but rather in a sort of constant apprehension lest he fall short of what is required. The distance between slave and master is to be acknowledged and expressed *in the simplicity of your heart.* Thus, slaves are to do their work without artifice, without constantly calculating; they are, if they have exerted themselves, to maintain the feeling that they could have done more. And this because they are to render obedience to their master *as Christ.* Christ is thus represented in a kind of substitution by the master according to the flesh, just as he was represented before by the husband and by the father. If slaves have simplicity of heart, they will recognize in their feeling of inadequacy what they owe to the Lord. Consequently, as slaves they have an advantage with respect to other Christians. Their relationship of service according to the flesh is drawn into their relationship of service to the divine Lord, and whatever they do while performing it is extended invisibly toward him. If they follow their master according to the flesh in fear and trembling, just as they would follow the Lord, this is a genuine following of the Lord. Slaves thus have the simplest way, that of humble earthly obedience, which as such becomes Christian obedience.

6:6. *Not performing eye service like those who would please men, but like slaves of Christ, fulfilling the will of God with your whole soul.*

When men do not look to God in their service, if they are not guided by the unconditioned character of Christian service, they slip into eye service and man pleasing. They serve only as long as they are supervised, and they will do only the indispensable minimum of what it is their obligation to do. Their interest is not directed toward service as such but toward their standing with their master and thus, when all is said and done, toward themselves. Paul's desire, however, is that slaves partake of the Lord's divine service, that they make as much of his disposition and his interest as possible, in order to serve more and more in his spirit, to place their service in his service, so that he may transform it into a part of his service of the Father. Everything temporal, calculated, and limited would then drop away by the grace of the Lord, because such things were never to be met with in his service. Because the Lord serves *with his whole soul* and slaves are drawn by faith into his service, they too will try to serve with their whole soul. Not only the objective performance will be useful for the Lord, but the spirit of the server himself will be impregnated by him.

6:7. *Serve willingly as if serving the Lord, not men.*

To serve willingly means to serve without inconstancy, persevering in a willingness that does not flinch from the full realism of the condition of service on earth and nevertheless has its origin from elsewhere, from above. Realism because a hard service is required of most men. If the masters are not believers, they will not consider their servants otherwise than as mere men, of whom diligence, but also negligence, is to be expected. If they counted on diligence alone, they would show that they expect more of their servants than can be expected of an ordinary man, that they have set a hope upon them that exceeds the human measure. But the attitude of masters is not of consequence at the moment. For slaves must serve willingly *as if serving the Lord*; with their eyes on the Lord, they are to try to satisfy the perhaps excessive expectation of the master. It is right if the masters recognize something in them that makes them conspicuous over and above the disposition and performance of ordinary men. An excessive demand was also placed on the Lord, and he performed something that, strictly speaking, could not be expected of a man. He draws upon this performance to show his servants how their task is to be discharged. That servants now serve their master as they serve the Lord is no empty fiction. The strength to serve that is given to them is the strength of the Lord, and their exercise of earthly service is real training in the service of the Lord. By the Christian "fiction", which sees the Lord in the earthly master, service becomes Christian, and then Christ can dispose of his servant at any time, because that servant has learned to serve and in serving has come to know the quality of the Lord's love.

6:8. *You know, in fact, that everyone who has done something good will receive it from the Lord, whether he be a slave or a freeman.*

Knowing accompanies work and shares in its law. Because every aspect of love strives toward the Lord, the Lord also gives us the grace to know that it is striving toward a goal. It is not as if the earthly worker pursued what to his mind were purely worldly aims while, unbeknown to him, the Lord stretched his work objectively into a supramundane context. The Lord does not leave his own in the dark concerning the sense of their work. Those who believe in him form a community of knowers, who do not construct their knowledge on the basis of mere conjectures but draw it wholly from the love of the Lord. Everyone receives it, whether *he be a slave or a freeman*. Everyone is recompensed by the Lord himself, wherein once again the distinction between slave and freeman plays no role. The relation of every individual to the Lord is always shaped in a personal manner, even though it is shaped within the community. But this relationship has a measure, which not only lies with the Lord but brings his recompense into relation with the performance of the individual. That he will recompense us according to the measure of our good deeds does not prevent his recompense from being total and free grace. For this reason we will not be able to survey this measure from above when the recompense is given. Thus, we must constantly re-entrust to the Lord the measure of our good, in order to summon without ceasing renewed courage by this entrusting; and yet, precisely in leaving the measure to the Lord, we submit ourselves to the law of his remuneration, which in a mysterious way makes use of this measure in order to be able, when the grace of the recompense arrives, to dispense with it more easily, thus making it superfluous, because in the end the recompense has its measure in the relationship of the Son to the Father.

6:9. *And you masters, do the same in their regard; stop threatening; knowing that their Lord and your Lord is in the heavens
and that with him there is no respect of persons.*

Finally, the Apostle addresses himself to masters; but he
speaks with them otherwise than with servants. To the
latter he shows the gradation of rank: they are under the
masters, the masters under Christ. But he does not show
masters their superiority over slaves; Christ alone is master, and they are all subject to him. Before him the lords
are placed on the same level as slaves: both serve, indeed,
from the Lord's point of view, they perform together a
single service. Masters too must know: the recompense
comes from the Lord and is pure grace. In their work
and in their willingness to be used, they must be dominated by this thought and for its sake forbear threatening.
They must know that their Lord is the same as the Lord
of their servants. It is he who recapitulates in himself all
service, that of masters as well as that of slaves, and brings
it into his one service before the Father; and in the face
of this unity, the insignificant gradation of rank between
slaves and masters falls away as something inconsequen-
tial, laughably small.

Since, for the sake of the masters, Paul insists so much
on their relationship as servants to the one Lord, masters
must no longer consider their lordship in relation to slaves
in any other way; they must no longer be able to derive
it from anywhere other than from their relationship of
service to the Lord. They serve the Lord by commanding
those subject to them, by taking their service into their
own, lifting it into their own responsibility and directing

the whole of it on to the Lord. For before the Lord *in the heavens*, who from that vantage point has the comprehensive vision of everything, *there is no respect of persons*. By the quality of his own performance before the Father, the Lord evaluates the quality of the work to be performed and already performed. Service is judged by service and not according to the person. Earth by heaven, master and slave by the Lord.

THE ARMOR OF GOD

6:10. *For the rest, brethren, be strengthened in the Lord and in the power of his might.*

Paul has concluded the principal part of his exhortations. What follows recapitulates and enlarges it once again in the sense that Paul makes everything flow into strength. Since God is almighty, Christians have no reason to grow weak or to let themselves go. All they have to do is unceasingly draw their strength where the source of all strength is, in God. For the work of the Lord increasingly demands such strength. A strength that is necessary to carry out the Lord's demands. The Lord can demand of man whatever he wants, because he himself makes available the strength to do it. Paul has a provided a comprehensive view of what is demanded; for the process itself, for its execution, and for the perseverance in what has been begun, he refers to the Lord, who never leaves anyone in the lurch, who keeps his entire divine power in readiness for man's use. The limits of what man is able to undertake and accomplish are expanded and, as it were, obliterated, since he can and must no longer reflect on how much lies within his power and what God can demand from him. He knows only that when he has undertaken something the Lord purposes, the Lord will give him the strength to bring it to completion precisely as he wishes.

Yet neither does Paul desire that we leave everything to the strength of the Lord; we are told to be *strengthened* ourselves. We are encouraged to make use of the strength of the Lord so that it may work in us and through us. The center of omnipotence, which center lies in the Lord, is so to say enlarged into those who are sent on a mission; there is a phase of strengthening themselves, of assimilating strength, and this phase lies in the very giving up of self, provided it is authentic. The Lord himself plants his strength in us so that it may bear fruit in us. And we have to feel and to suffer exertion, effort, every adversity in work, within a service demanded and assigned by him.

6:11. *Put on the full armor of God, so that you may be able to stand firm against the snares of the devil.*

It is the same old situation: man between God and the devil, who lies in ambush for man when he is engaged with God. God had shown man the weapons against the devil: love of God and, in love, the keeping of the commandments, the avoidance of what was forbidden. If Adam had loved God sufficiently, he would have had enough weapons against the devil. After man has fallen into sin, and as a redeemed believer carries in himself the aftereffects of sin, the devil has even more points of assault than in paradise. For this reason God fits man out with full *armor*. Only God does not give these weapons once and for all into man's possession. For it is *God's* own weapons that man may make use of, the same weapons the Lord himself used when he was tempted by the devil. Every proven weapon of the God-man: weapons of God and weapons of man. For what God the Son made trial of he proved as man. The fact that he uses them or lends them to man takes away nothing of their divine power, but they are fitted to man, and this adjustment takes place in faith. Faith allows man to use God's weapons as his own, in the lasting awareness that they are God's personal property, lent to him for the fight against the devil. *So that you may be able to stand firm.* The Christian wills to stand firm. He wills this because only by standing firm does he stand so as to be able to stand on God's side. As soon as he does not stand firm against the devil, he ceases to stand in God's presence. But in order to stand in God's presence, he must seek from God everything necessary to do so and must use it according to God's intention. He must not turn the weapons gradually into his own, in the opinion that he and his weapons together made up the power capable of resisting the devil. There is in the devil an antidivine power that only God himself can conquer with the power found in the grace of his weapons, in the weapons of his grace.

6:12. *For we have to fight, not against flesh and blood, but against the principalities and the powers, against the world rulers of this present darkness, against the spiritual powers of wickedness in the heavenly places.*

Against flesh and blood we ourselves can fight; there is, as it were, no need of the whole supernatural armor in order to move against the natural assaults that lie in us. Faith and its strength are enough here to secure conquest, faith in the sense of the general foundation Paul takes for granted in his epistle. *But against the principalities and the powers, against the world rulers of this present darkness*, against every evil thing that not only wages battle against us but is in battle against God himself. Because they are primarily enemies of God, they are secondarily our foes as well, with whom we would perhaps have nothing to do if we had not taken God's part, if we had not decided to place our whole lives in God's service, if we had not risked being on God's side and considering his enemies our most personal foes. The battle Paul has in mind here is the battle for God's cause. The demonic power is everywhere on the scene where God should be and where he is, even *in the heavenly places*. Not only in the narrow and personal affairs of men, but also in the principles of creation. It is in the heavenly places, in God's high places, that the communication Christ-Church takes place, the realization of God's plans by the saints and all those who have a commission, in fine, theology itself. The enemies of God can also try to interfere with God's plans and thwart the plans of the saints in heaven, who, so long as the sinful world endures, are also unable to carry through everything they desire. Even things of which we are unaware, because they are too close to God, can be accessible to the devil and can be attacked by him. It is against this devil that we have to fight. Against everything that belongs to the realm of *darkness*, even if it goes beyond our concepts and our own selves. Thus, our readiness must also be much greater than we can measure ourselves, for we never know when we are drawn into the transcendent mysteries of God or the mysteries of the devil. The closer we come to God and the deeper the things we perceive of him, the more do we learn of the devil as well and survey his workings.

6:13. *Take up therefore the full armor of God, so that on the evil day you can resist and in everything remain perfectly steadfast.*

What is true of faith is analogously true of God's weapons: one cannot select; one cannot take up an eclectic position. One must not merely make oneself entirely available from the very outset but must also undertake everything God proposes. It is God himself who places his weapons at one's disposition; and even though he differentiates them for us, they nonetheless form a whole, a unitary armor. We all know sin; and it too in its differentiations is a whole. None of us can say that a particular sin can exercise no attraction on us so that there is a determinate weapon of God we would not need. As we always have to be vigilant in the whole, since we are aware of our weakness, so too we must be grateful for every weapon and take it up. *So that on the evil day you can resist.* The evil day is as if in suspension in this statement of Paul; neither its moment in time nor its content is more precisely described, nor even, despite the singular, its number. It is the day of temptation, the day when we can fall, and this day can repeat itself. But it can also, if we are vigilant by grace and have the weapons of God to resist, pass by without harm. One thing only is certain: no one will remain protected from temptation; but it is also certain that no believer will be refused God's weapons. If we have *remained steadfast*, we are not dispensed from the duty of continuing to stand fast as well. It is not the case that, because we have overcome once, every danger is removed from us, that, because we have won one victory, we have already shown ourselves perfectly *steadfast*. Even after victory we must remain fighters and ever and again expect the evil day ahead of us.

6:14. *Stand, then, girded about your loins with truth and clothed with the breastplate of righteousness.*

Paul now presupposes that the command to take up the weapons—which is at the same time to hold them fast—has been obeyed and goes on to the description of the armor. The first thing he demands is the girding of the *loins with truth*. Since the truth belongs to God alone, since he is truth and bestows truth upon us, the first thing is an abiding within the truth of God. An abiding God himself gives by granting us his truth in which to remain fully and with which to gird ourselves. This truth thus gives us holding power, which makes it easy for us to defend ourselves, inasmuch as we have to hold, not some truth we have thought up ourselves, but that truth which in itself is a weapon and strength. The strength of God's truth passes into the one who has to stand in it. It is not as if we had to translate God's truth by some sort of exertion into human truth in order to be able to defend it, in order to be able, as it were, to give it a strength in the world, in order to press into its hand weapons with which it can defend itself. It is rather the reverse: the Christian has to remain standing in the truth of God, which is weapon enough to defend itself and the Christian at the same time, provided the Christian really uses it as a weapon and fights. *Clothed with the breastplate of righteousness.* We are to clothe ourselves, to mantle ourselves with the gifts of God. We are not in any sense to absorb them into ourselves but to conserve their divine character and their integrity, and our integrity within theirs. So that, when one comes upon someone clothed with the breastplate of righteousness, the first thing one notices about him is the righteousness of God and only afterward the man who wears it. This is the instruction given us so that we may stand firm on the evil day: that God's gift becomes the primary thing in us and that we ourselves become secondary. The believer has to take up and reflect untouched, unadulterated, unbroken, both the truth and the righteousness of God; and in the mediation of the divine gifts to the world, he appears only as the obedient servant who remains behind the gifts as one hidden and unnoticed. Yet he is to stand with his whole personality in the armor because it is expected that he and no other fight with these weapons. The weapons do not violate him. They only make him what he is supposed to be, a soldier of God.

6:15. *And shod with the readiness of the gospel of peace.*

The whole man has to be at God's disposal, along with everything he has, plans, and does. In fact, he must surround what he possesses of himself with what the Lord gives him. The Lord gives the *gospel*, the message *of peace*. He does not give it to man as if it were intended for his sole and exclusive use; rather, it takes from him its starting point; it passes in him and through him back into the

Church and the world. The gospel of peace can continue to exist only if it can effect in the individual what the Lord expects. And this is service. Service that is a derivative of his service before the Father. It is this that the gospel of peace is intended to disseminate, by traveling from man to man, from country to country. But it can do this only with the help of those who believe, and it thus communicates itself to them as a sort of *message*, ready to take effect just as the Lord wishes. The one who believes, who takes it up, must clothe himself about with this message; and if this clothing is portrayed here as being shod, this is because it is readiness to communicate, which comes from the gospel and must be spread together with it.

6:16. *In all these things, taking up the shield of faith, with which you are able to extinguish all the fiery darts of the enemy.*

The darts come from the enemy, and they not only have the effect of projectiles that wound but do something beyond this: they also burn and ignite as well. Which means that the one who comes under attack must cover and defend not only himself but also what belongs to him. This is what belongs to the Lord and to all believers. When the Lord gives us faith, love, and hope, this gift is indeed meant personally for us but at the same time is always also given for the whole community of believers. We have to take care that it lives not only in us but in all those to whom the Lord in his love has made the divine gift. Now Paul says that we should take up *the shield of faith*, the weapon with which we not only have the power to intercept the darts but are also permitted to extinguish them.

This applies to *all these things*. All of the foregoing: truth, justice, and readiness must be put into practice in such a way that faith is the reality that encompasses them. Hitherto, the full armor was required so that man could endure. It now becomes manifest that he has to fight against determinate weapons of the devil, weapons that ricochet off of faith without any effect. Faith is here like the recapitulation of all the foregoing gifts of God and a new strengthening of them. Like the sum of everything so far, which at the same time adds a new element. It is also as if one had to take up a special weapon for every particular occasion and as if, in spite of that, every temptation contained in turn one principal intention: to make faith fall. Both in the offense and in the defense, the particular and the general can be seen in every case.

6:17. *And take up the helmet of salvation and the sword of the spirit, which is the Word of God.*

If it is true that the Christian can, in Paul's mind, stand his ground only by attacking, can repulse evil only by carrying out apostolic activity, then it is also clear that he cannot do without the Word of God as a weapon. The Word of God always works apostolically; even in one who already believes, it introduces him more deeply into his faith. If a believer recognizes the Word of God in himself, then he knows immediately that he absolutely must actively serve this Word, in a service of obedience but also one of transmission of the Word. An inherent trait of the working of the Word in man is that it immediately demands of him further working: to be carried to others.

Paul distinguishes two aspects of this Word. He speaks first of the *helmet of salvation*. This category is reserved to the Son, who is the head of the Church. It is his prerogative to strengthen the head of the believer. But the Son, as the one sent by the Father, was on earth the bearer *of the Spirit*, and the Spirit made his word a *sword*. The Son and the Spirit always find themselves united in the word of the gospel, of salvation, that the Father sends out. At the beginning of the description of the armor, the Father seemed to be predominantly the one who made the weapons available. Now it is more the Son in his unity with the Spirit who offers himself as the Word to be a weapon, in order to confer impact upon his truth. At the beginning, Paul commended the full armor of God. Then he described the single weapons and once again summed them up in faith. In this summary it becomes clear in turn that faith is offered to us by all three Persons of God. Hence, we cannot make a selection as to the weapon, either in faith and its apostolate or in God. We must always call upon the triune God for help and serve him just as he gives himself to us.

6:18. *Offer at all times through the Spirit every sort of prayer and supplication. Be vigilant in them in all perseverance and in prayer for all the saints.*

There is not, then, one time for prayer and then other time. For the Christian, there is only the time of the Lord, before whom he continually stands and in whose *Spirit* he lives. Everything the Spirit suggests to him is also a component of prayer. He is told to offer *every sort of prayer and supplication*, but only that which is prompted by the Spirit. The Spirit requires of him an attitude, and when he lives in this attitude, the Spirit suggests to him the necessary words by which he can pray and adore God in a way consonant with the Son. And this is *at all times*, for the Spirit does not cease to place him before the Father.

Be vigilant in them. Vigilance will prevent the Christian from falling out of prayer. This vigilance has to be realized *in all perseverance*, so that the Spirit may always find him in the required attitude and prayer may always remain his prayer. The Christian is to persevere *in prayer for all the saints*, for all who have become holy by faith, for all whom the Lord invites to enter into his communion and to whom he gives a commission within it. Every prayer in the Spirit must strengthen the communion of saints, working like a hammer to fasten the pray-er more firmly to this communion and the communion more firmly to God.

6:19. *For me as well, so that when I open my mouth the word will be given me, to announce boldly the mystery of the gospel.*

Paul needs the prayer of the community and asks them for it. Not primarily so that the fruit of their prayer may take effect in him, but so that he may do what God has required of him: announce *the mystery of the gospel* in the right way. It has to happen *boldly*, that is, without clouding the message on account of any regard for his own

person. He must be able to confess free from himself
and with courage, without heeding obstacles or thinking
of dangers. *The mystery of the gospel* is the same as that
of the Lord, it contains everything the Lord brings from
heaven by his Incarnation. It is essentially mystery, to
however great an extent it is announced. A mystery of
faith, of hope, and of love into which, so long as we are
on earth, we are allowed glimpses here and there. But
it is all the more necessary that these cursory views be
objective according to the intention of the Lord and not
clouded by human considerations. If Paul's doctrine of
prayer ascribes everything to the Holy Spirit, he knows
that even the effect is left to the Holy Spirit but also that
he, Paul, because he believes and is sent, must belong to
this effect. The Spirit will thus make himself known both
at the origin of prayer as well as when it takes effect in the
Apostle. Everyone who is willing to do what the Spirit
requires of him can commend himself in this prayer. All
believers, along with their whole capacity to will and to
attempt what God awaits from them, are here included in
this obedience to the Spirit, in a dedication that includes
and assents to everything God the Father gives to man in
the Son by the Holy Spirit and expects from him as the
fruit of this gift.

6:20. *For which I am an ambassador in chains, and so that I
may be emboldened to speak as I must.*

Paul is an *ambassador*, that is, he is entrusted with a personal mission, which is permanent and definitive. He will
have it as long as he lives and can work actively. He sees

it in the proclamation of the word. He is sent in the strength of the Father, of the Son, and of the Holy Spirit to transmit, after having received it, the message the Son brought with himself. This content of his mission is just as final as the mission itself. But he is an ambassador *in chains*; he is hindered from freely exercising his task. Nevertheless, his mission is ultimately not affected by his imprisonment. It continues unbroken in him. The chains in no way mean a release from his commission. He cannot loose his chains. But he must not cease to announce the mystery of the gospel. He does not doubt this present commission for a moment. The base from which he can now preach is restricted, as is, for that reason, his effective range. The commission remains. The brethren are asked to pray *so that I may be emboldened to speak as I must*. So that no gulf opens up between the apprehension and the exercise of the mission and so that he may not let himself be so upset by his destiny that it makes him forget his mission. He has to proclaim two things: the word as well as the survival of his mission, so that the community may understand that his chains have no influence upon either. Because this requires maintaining before God and man the unity between mission and execution, the Apostle needs the prayer of the community. He has already instructed the community in the weapons of God. Now he himself needs these weapons. Prayer appears as the highest weapon he wants the community to place at his disposition through the Spirit. He thus knows clearly and absolutely about the existence of intercession.

6:21. *But so that you too may know how things are going with me and what I am doing, Tychicus, beloved brother and faithful servant in the Lord, will announce everything to you.*

Paul has instructed the community up until now about how things are to go with it and what it has to do. At a certain point he can no longer do that without announcing to it as well how it goes with him and what he is doing. It is part of his office to busy himself with all who believe. But they have the right to know how it fares with those who attend them. They have to live the truths preached to them in a sort of eternity, but in exchange they have the right to be solicitous for the temporal concerns of the preacher. They have received his truth as an entirely ministerial one but have in exchange the right to be worried about his personal welfare. A part of the Apostle's message consisted in caring for the community, so that the Apostle cannot withdraw himself from its care for him. He has instructed it in how it has to grow in its communion, and in exchange it is entitled to grow in communion with him.

The one who is going to inform the community about him is the *beloved brother Tychicus*, one who is bound by his office both to the Apostle and to the community. He knows how the Apostle is doing, not merely by chance, but because he has seen it and, still more, because he is the *faithful servant in the Lord*, who knows about Paul not only as a friend but also on account of his office. The official character of his life, his existence in the Lord, and the ministry shared with Paul allow him a true judgment about the situation and state of the Apostle. He conveys the news in a mission that has an affinity with the mission of the Apostle. The appellations *beloved* and *faithful* bring out this genuine correlation in order to underscore with greater emphasis the veracity of Tychicus.

6:22. *Whom I have sent to you for this purpose, so that you may learn how we are doing and he may console your hearts.*

The community, when it learns of Paul's chains, will be anxious. Paul would like this apprehension to preserve the right Christian character. For this reason he sends them this friend, so that he may inform them and at the same time console them. It is not said that the content of the news conveyed by him will be of a consoling character. Yet Paul wants to console his people, giving them his own consolation. He has the consolation of one who serves and who places his service before his life. Tychicus, the faithful servant, likewise has this consolation and can bring it to the community. His consolation has an official character, and the community, relying on its faith, has to adjust itself to the office in such a way that it really allows itself to be consoled, that it understands the motives for consolation and, strengthened by them, lives as a consoled community.

6:23. *Peace to the brethren and love together with faith from God the Father and from the Lord Jesus Christ.*

Peace, love, and faith are three goods Paul sends to the community at the end. All three come from God and are therefore freighted with divine qualities and have to be accepted by the community if it is to be able to carry into effect a divine activity within it. Then they are what remains in the end. The letter Paul has written has shown many possible ways for Christians. He ends by letting everything, including Paul, the preacher and exhorter, disappear into the gifts that come directly from God—peace, love, faith—indeed, into the unity of these gifts just as they exist in God. All together they are like a single gift that permanently flows out of God, that both joins the Father with the Son and flows down from them upon men as from a common source. These gifts coming out of the relationship of the Father and the Son have been in them from eternity and are eternally placed at the disposition of every individual who lives in faith and dares to attempt to accept the entire teaching of the Son. They lose nothing of their eternal power by coming from heaven to individual men. *Peace* is like the first notion that includes the others in itself. The *brethren* can possess peace only when they have *love*, and they can love only in *faith*. The differentiation of the one gift is due to men, who can receive it thus and not otherwise. In God himself it is perfect unity. The demarcations are manifested in us in order to make the path of unity easier for us and to make the goal more alluring, so that we may strengthen and deepen our faith and let it be tried more and more by God and, by these means, may grow into greater love, which will bring us to deeper peace.

6:24. *Grace be with all who love our Lord Jesus Christ in imperishability. Amen.*

Grace is now no longer something coming from the Father, passing through the Son, distributed by the Spirit, but only grace, grace in the absolute sense, grace pure and simple. It is desired for and bestowed upon all *who love our Lord Jesus Christ in imperishability.* For this love comprises every love as well as the whole of faith. Because this love is an all-inclusive, perfect love, it has to be in *imperishability,* to remain freighted with this eternal property of the triune divine love, like to itself at every moment and through all ages. Grace is invoked upon those who love in this manner. Grace can only be if it is bound to those who love in this way, bound by the love of God, who binds himself in order to be in all who love. God gives love and gives grace as a gift that is meant to be in all who love, and grace encounters in them love, which is also God's gift. The believers are the point of intersection between the perfect grace of God and the perfect, incorruptible, imperishable love of God. This is the blessing that it is Paul's privilege to send to his own in the name of the triune God.